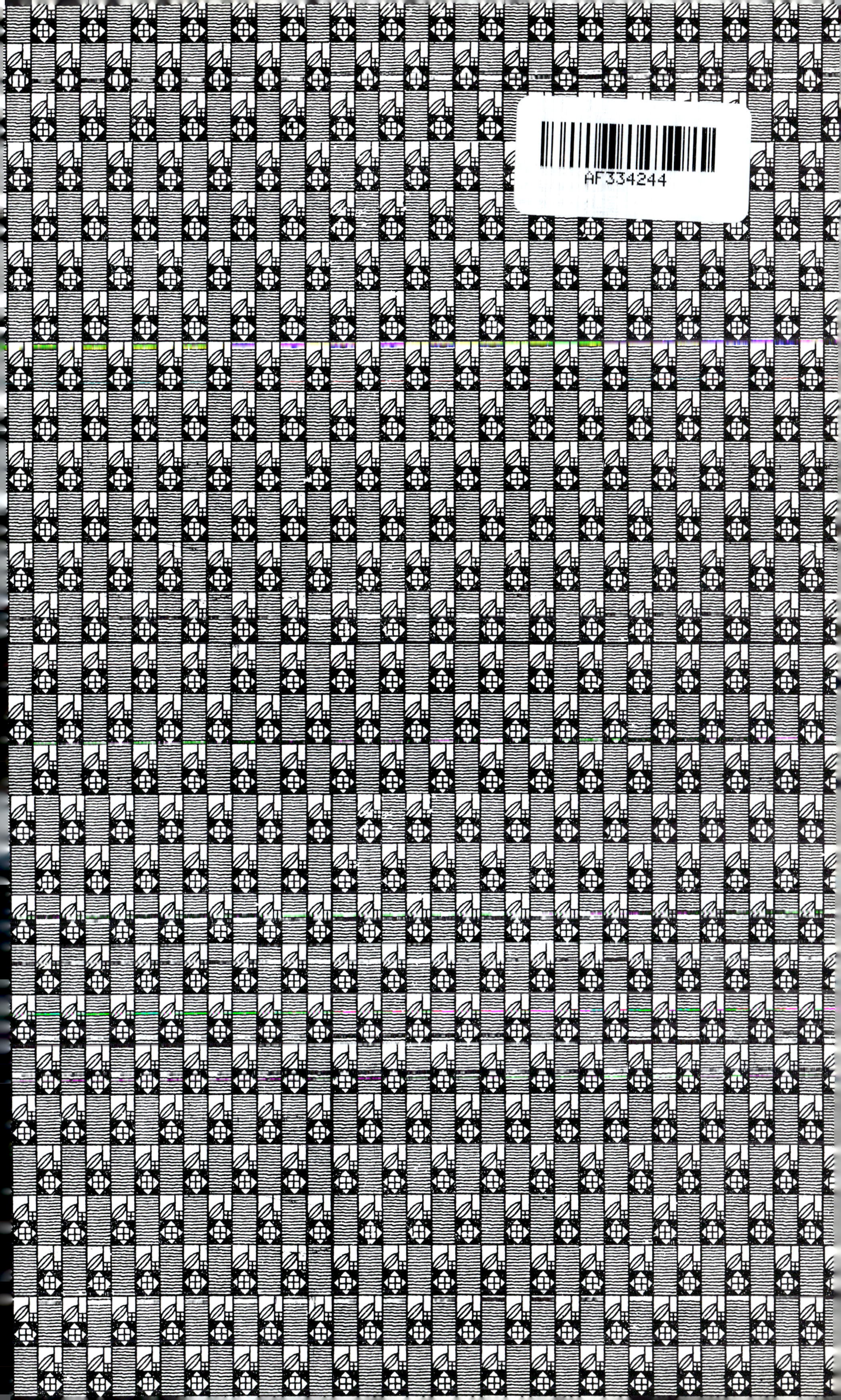
AF334244

SECESSIONISM and Austrian Graphic Art 1900—1920

SECESSIONISM

and Austrian Graphic Art 1900—1920
From the Collection of the Neue Galerie der Stadt Linz · SITES

Organized by the Smithsonian Traveling Exhibition Service

Catalogue: edited and designed by Peter Baum

The Smithsonian Institution Traveling Exhibition Service (SITES) is especially pleased to bring to United States audiences *Secessionism and Austrian Graphic Art (1900—1920): From the Collection of the Neue Galerie der Stadt Linz*. This exhibition includes an important body of drawings, prints and watercolors that illustrate the extent to which Secessionist artists challenged established conventions, not only artistically, but also socially and politically.

Secessionism and Austrian Graphic Art was selected jointly by Prof. Peter Baum, Director, Neue Galerie der Stadt Linz, and Donald McClelland, Exhibition Coordinator and Curator, SITES. Peter Baum's penetrating essay and his catalogue entries will make this publication an essential reference for the study of Austrian art during the early twentieth century.

It is a pleasure to acknowledge the cooperation and assistance of the Austrian government, particularly the Embassy of Austria in Washington, D.C., for consenting to act as patron of the exhibition during its United States tour. International exhibitions require expertise in many areas, and dedication and enthusiasm at every stage. Chemie Holding AG supported *Secessionism and Austrian Graphic Art* with a generous grant. Austrian Airlines is serving as the official carrier of the exhibition. The Austrian Cultural came forth with generous assistance on the catalogue, and the Federal Ministry for Science and Research has made itself available to this project from its inception.

Special recognition also is extended to staff at the Smithsonian Institution Traveling Exhibition Service. Linda Bell, Assistant Director for Administration; Lee Williams, Head Registrar; Andrea Stevens, Publications Director: Marci Silverman, Exhibition Assistant: Gregory Naranjo and Katherine Hudgens, Consultants; and Melissa Hallman, Intern all played essential roles in bringing *Secessionism and Austrian Graphic Art* to fruition.

The directors and our colleagues at participating museums have offered counsel and cooperation at every step of the way, for which we are especially grateful.

Anna R. Cohn
Director, Smithsonian Institution Traveling Exhibition Service

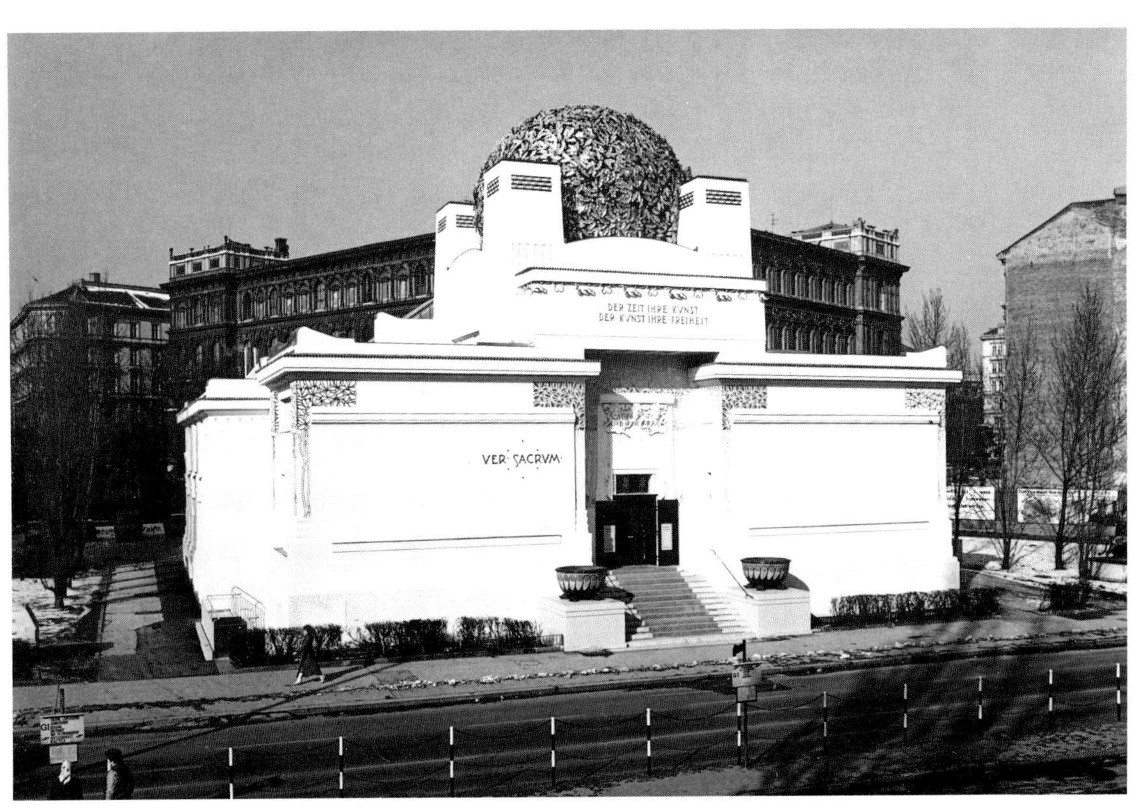

The Vienna Secession Building today, Photo: Margherita Krischanitz, Vienna

"To the age its art. To art its freedom."

inscription on Vienna's Secessionist building, 1898

During the declining years of the Habsburg Empire an amazing group of artists burst upon the Austrian cultural scene. Mahler, Schönberg, Webern, Klimt, Schiele, Kokoschka, Otto Wagner, and Adolf Loos, all of them destined to enter the pantheon of modern art, emerged in this fertile artistic milieu. Even today, after a lapse of almost one hundred years, one still feels something of the excitement of the period through its art. Many of the works reflect a newfound freedom to explore the human mind, with its dreams, its contradictions, and its richness of true emotion. Vienna, the center of this creative maelstrom, was after all where Sigmund Freud had begun to probe the uncharted realm of the subconscious.

Above all, however, the artists of the Secessionist movement sought freedom from the forceful rule of the art establishment. Many believed that the Academy's focus on heroic portraiture and the glorification of the state was a betrayal of the modern age. Like their counterparts in other cities of the German-speaking world such as Munich and Berlin, a small group of Viennese artists decided that they would no longer tolerate the reactionary policies of Vienna's semi-official Society of Artists and declared in April of 1897 their intention to form an independent exhibition society. The new society, "Secession", took its name from the revolt.

The Secessionists' aim was two-fold: to bring about a heightened concern for art in Vienna and to bring Viennese and other Austrian artists into more lively contact with art from abroad. These aims were to be achieved through exhibitions to which foreign artists (known as "corresponding members") would contribute and through the publication of the Society's magazine, *Ver Sacrum.*

The magazine's title, derived from the Latin for "sacred spring", alludes to the ancient Roman ritual of consecrating youth at a spring in times of natural danger. The Secessionist group defined itself not merely as a *salon des réfusés* but also as a kind of new Roman order inspired by classical ideals while at the same time rejecting their misuse by the old patricians. It is perhaps surprising that in the midst of this revolutionary fervor one sees a new veneration of Vienna's classical heritage. This was fostered, in all probability, by the era's love of the exotic. Ancient Greece and Rome (like the newly "discovered" Orient) were the focus of much fascination in the popular mind, because of the archeological finds of the day. However, it was the spirit of classical art, as much as its surface, that gave sustenance to many of these artists. Greek and Roman sculptors had established a tradition of looking at the individual's human qualities, replete with frailties as well as ambitions. Inner thoughts and feelings — essence rather than image, true self rather than ideal — found expression in their work. Vienna's artists did not slavishly copy the art of Greece and Rome, but rather strove to create from it a new idiom without losing sight of the old.

The democratic institutions of the classical world were also sources of inspiration. The Secessionists were in complete agreement with the new concept of bringing the arts

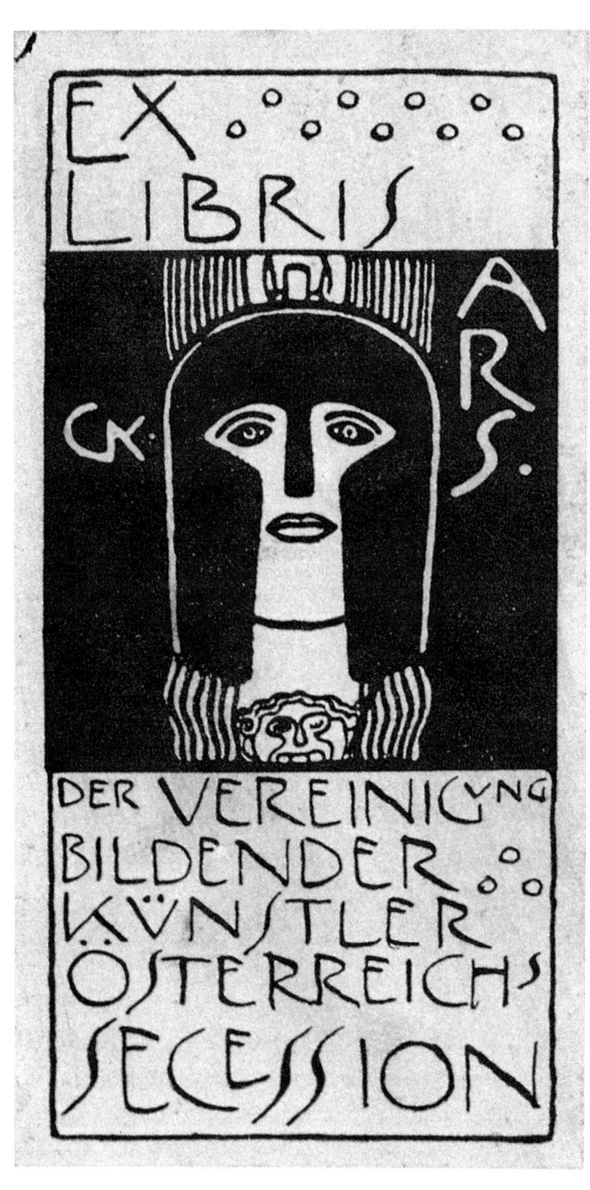

Ex Libris by Gustav Klimt

down from their pedestal and merging them into everyday life. No longer was painting the highest form of expression: now, distinctions were not to be made between "high" art and "low". The graphic arts in particular were viewed with new interest, for they were a means of bringing art to everyone. As if to emphasize this point, the fifth Secession exhibition, in 1899, was devoted exclusively to drawings and prints. Today, it is difficult to see how truly revolutionary this act was, but surely to the Academy an exhibition of the graphic arts — disdained as a popular art form — must have been a travesty.

The fifth exhibition presented a range of not only contemporary Austrian graphics but also those from elsewhere in Europe. We can observe how Austrian artists of the time responded to specific foreign work represented at this and later Secessionist exhibitions. American James McNeill Whistler (1834—1903), Belgian Fernand Khnopff (1858—1921), and Englishman Aubrey Beardsley (1872—1898) — all corresponding members of the Secessionists — were received with great enthusiasm. The graphic artists in the present exhibition embraced the foreign influences, which reflected a new sense of vision in the use of line, color, and form to convey the essence of nature and human feelings. Across Europe, the possibilities for each of these ingredients of art were being furiously re-examined. The Impressionists, for their part, expanded the expressive possibilities of color, carried to the extreme by Van Gogh. With Seurat, color and form achieved total harmony. With Cezanne, form was created out of color. Line, pure line, as found in the black and white calligraphy of Chinese and Islamic inscriptions, inspired many. Few understood the inscriptions, but the exotic abstract forms appealed to the imagination. Japanese prints in particular provided a source of design strange to Western culture yet somehow structurally logical.

Gustav Klimt (1862—1918), the absolute leader of the Secessionists and the most eclectic among them, absorbed an extraordinary variety of these influences. His world was one of opulent color, sensuality, emotional subtlety, and fantasy. Klimt, who began his career as an academic painter of considerable talent, went on to find favor among Vienna's new society of merchants, bankers, and professionals. He decorated their drawing rooms with gleaming panels of gold and silver and portraits of beautiful, dreaming women with overtones of mysticism.

The standing full-length figures often seen in his paintings and drawings might be compared to those portraits painted by Whistler where line and silhouette express a heightened sense of importance. The 1901 drawing of Frau von Rosthorn (Figure 27), a favorite Viennese singer, reveals Klimt's love of line and his ability to draw as almost second nature. Frau von Rosthorn's dress may have been designed by Klimt and could have been acquired at the Viennese fashion house of his sister-in-law Helene Flöge. *Seated Woman* (Figure 28), clothed in the latest Klimt-like fashion, possesses a subtle sensuality that gives line a life of its own as we almost subconsciously attempt to trace its beginning to its end.

Khnopff significantly influenced Klimt with his idealist and individualistic thoughts. Idealism, as explained by Khnopff, was a desire to find the perfection of reality beyond history and nature. This concept appealed to Klimt, as can be seen in his landscapes and particularly in his portraiture.

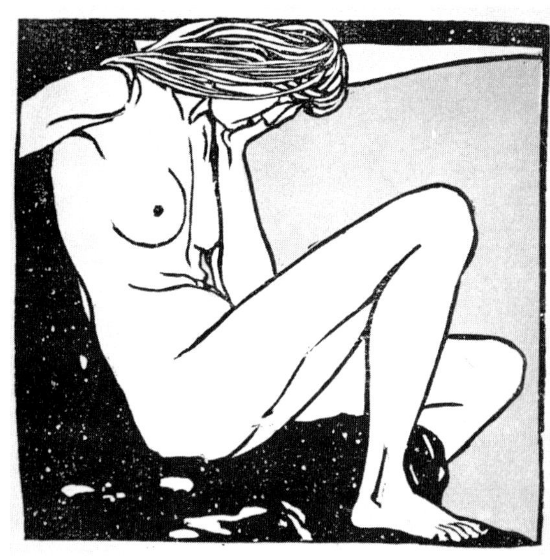

Woodcut by Maximilian Kurzweil, Edition of Ver Sacrum, 1903

The graphic artist Aubrey Beardsley also mirrored Klimt's views. Surely, Klimt was influenced by Beardsley's involvement with *The Yellow Book,* Britain's publication that closely paralleled *The Sacred Spring.* The mark of Beardsley's frieze-like drawings can be seen in Klimt's monumental *Beethoven Frieze* of 1902 and in his concern for detail however small or curious. Certainly the fragmental quality of the classical frieze, whose elements speak singly as well as in unison, must have appealed to both artists, who by their work must have spurred similar interests among others. In the prints of this exhibition, both in color and in monochrome, the tendency was to make mosaics of individual forms. Here decoration ist achieved not by drawing alone and the background is seldom reserved for empty space. Often, each part of a print maintains its own identity, even as it is subtly matched and balanced by others.

Odilon Redon (1840—1916), another formidable influence among the Secessionists, wrote in his *Journals:* "Black is the most essential of all colors . . . it draws its excitement and vitality from deep and secret sources . . . Nothing can debauch it." There is in the *Male Nude* of Egon Schiele (1890—1918), a black-and-white lithograph produced in 1912 (Figure 65), a sense of brutality — an almost savage and merciless scrutiny of the model, who may indeed be the artist himself. Along with this strain of brutality, however, there exists an element of compassion. We see the nude figure clothed in his own tragic state devoid of the trappings of life and station. Schiele's graphic and erotic poses ran into conflict with the establishment, distorting to some extent the general perception of his work. Yet what Freud called „its misunderstood and much maligned erotic" is but one element of Schiele's art. The artist's tragic early death robbed Austrian art of one of its most significant and only partially fulfilled talents.

Oskar Kokoschka (1886—1980), like so many of his contemporaries, experimented in a wide variety of different media. In the years before 1914, he was highly respected not only for his drawings, paintings, and prints but also for his poetry, plays, and essays.

In 1906 Kokoschka completed a book titled *Die Träumenden Knaben (The Dreaming Youths).* Its two black-and-white and eight colored lithographs, five of which can be seen in this exhibition, were printed by two Viennese printers: Chwala (who also printed the text) and Berger. Notably, the book carried a dedication to his teacher, Gustav Klimt. *The Dreaming Youths* was intended as an illustrated children's book with accompanying color lithographs. Kokoschka by his own account did not really adhere to the original idea but created instead an account in words and pictures of "my spiritual state at the time" — a sort of free-versification in pictures.

There are many, varied images and views expressed by the Austrian artists of the Secession, and they shifted from reality to dream and from the imaginary to the ordinary with the greatest of ease. This diversity is one of the incontestable strengths of the age. It was an era driven by the search for new ideas, coupled with an equally intense commitment to craft. In many works, the qualities of daring and perfection are carefully, delicately, perfectly balanced, creating a precise linear rhythm of line and color. Whether an illusion of reality or a more natural view of the landscape, these penetrating works bring us startlingly close to a world that has disappeared but that, through its art, lives on to inspire us all.

Donald McClelland
Exhibition Coordinator and Curator

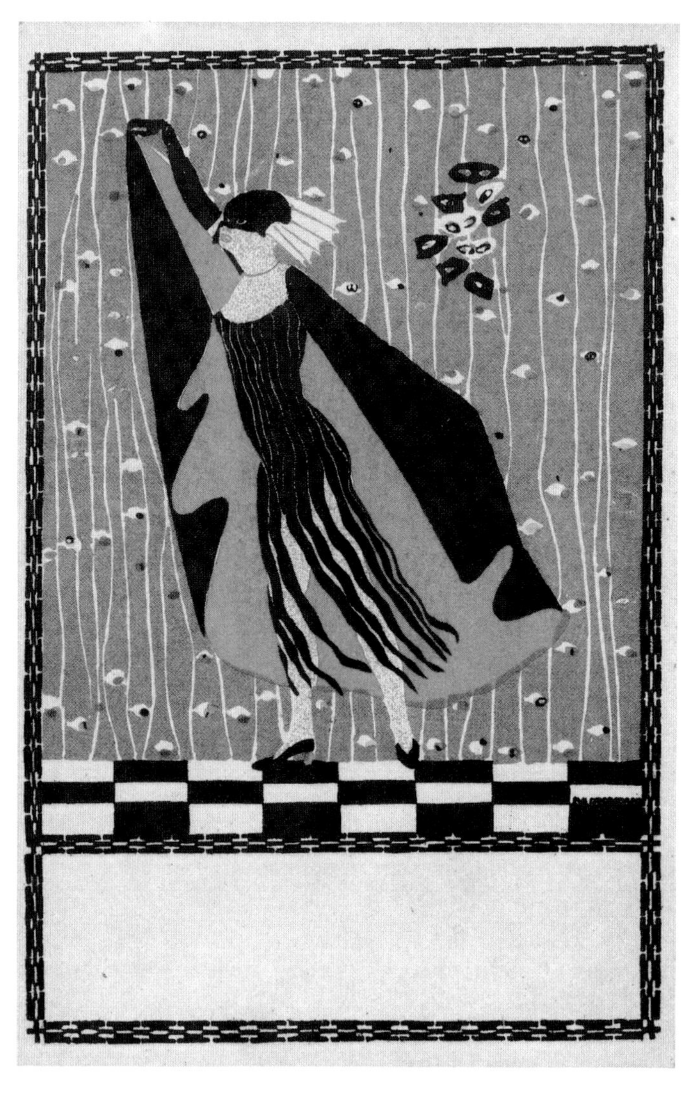

Mela Koehler, postcard of the Wiener Werkstätte

At the very beginning of the "classical" Modern period, with the general rise and forward thrust of visual arts around the turn of the century, at the very latest, graphic arts, within the development in Austria, take a leading position. In very nearly all the outstanding artists of the era — first and formost with Klimt, Schiele, and Kokoschka — we can observe a decisive and consistent interaction between their painting and their drawings and other graphic work. Even though, over the time range covered by our exhibit — 1900 to 1920 — one-of-a-kind graphics, and, within this category, mostly drawings, clearly dominate, and thus confirm their undisputed significance, the spectrum of print media in their great variety should neither be underestimated nor cast aside. Etching, engraving, dry-point, lithograph, woodcut, block print, linocut — all of these techniques at that time were used in innovative ways by more than just a few artists. Even in spite of lack of a market on today's scale, they still were printed, albeit in small or very small numbers. It turned out that, in the early decades of this century, graphic arts soon became the ideal sanctuary for artistic experiments of every kind — a sanctuary of the creative imagination, so to speak, — and certainly not only in Austria.

In keeping with the inclinations, tendencies, and strivings of the Secession movement at the "Wiener Kunstgewerbeschule" (Vienna School of Arts and Crafts, which later was to become the "Hochschule für angewandte Kunst" or College of Applied Arts) at the Stubenring, as well as of a similar trend at the "Wiener Werkstätte", graphic work became the focus of a meeting, confluence, and interaction between applied arts and non-utilitarian visual arts.

The high — and, at the same time, highly original standard of Vienna's applied graphic arts, their typographical peculiarities and decorative nature, became milestones of sophisticated design that were eventually appropriated — if you only think of the germinal and influential posters of the early Secession period — not only by those graphic artists involved in type styles, fonts, an new scripts, but also by leading painters and graphic artists in the field at large.

The general upsurge of fine arts, and a certain receptive openness in one's own country — the huge Danubian Dual Monarchy that was still intact at that time — but equally an orientation towards international standards, as practiced chiefly by the Secession in its exhibition policy, were decisive factors in a cultural climate that permitted the arts to prosper.

As for art education and the training of young artists, the very center of all progressive endeavors, as well as of the trend towards the "Gesamtkunstwerk", the total, encompassing, and unified work of art — a concept of special concern especially to the architects Josef Hoffmann and Koloman Moser — was the "Wiener Kunstgewerbeschule" that had been founded in 1867. From its very beginnings, this great educational institution had been closely tied to the "Museum für Kunst und Industrie" (Museum of Fine Arts and Industry) founded in 1864. Today, this collection still exists and is known as the "österreichische Museum für angewandte Kunst" (Austrian Museum of Applied Arts).

Apart from Hoffman (1870 to 1956) and Moser (1868 to 1918), most of the outstanding members of the teaching faculty of the "Kunstgewerbeschule" were artists specializing in one of the graphic media. They taught painting and drawing, drawing and painting of nudes, design, as well as print- and applied (or commercial) graphics. Alfred Roller (1864 — 1935), Erich Mallina (1873 — 1954), Carl Otto Czeschka (1878 — 1960), and Berthold Löffler (1874 — 1960), with whom Oskar

Kokoschka studied when he was a young man, are perhaps the ones to be emphasized for their particular influence on style formation and for the vast diversity of stimuli they gave their students.

The "Kunstgewerbeschule", which existed under its original name until 1918, exerted, at the very beginning of the Modern period in Vienna, which today commands worldwide interest and attention, a much more decisive influence than the older — and comparatively conservative — "Akademie der bildenden Künste" (Academy of Fine Arts).

At the turn of the century, Vienna still was the capital of one of the world's major powers, numbered more than two million inhabitants, and, having left Historism and the building boom of the Ringstrasse behind, became the scene of a new, individualistic rather than collective, flourishing of architecture, as attested by names like Otto Wagner, Adolf Loos, and Josef Hoffmann. A new, liberal, upper-crust bourgeoisie was open and receptive to all that was now emerging, and, at the same time, knew how to live in style.

The artists' collective of the Secession had been founded on April 3, 1897, for the purpose of making a clean break from the "Genossenschaft Bildender Künstler, Wiener Künstlerhaus", which they regarded as too conservative. Not much later, on November 12, 1898, to be exact, they moved into their functionally furnished new gallery building on Vienna's Naschmarkt. It had been designed by the young architect Joseph Maria Olbrich. Gustav Klimt was their first president, and the famous and generally widely esteemed water color painter and graphic artist Rudolf von Alt became their honorary president.

Under the programmatic title "Ver Sacrum" (Holy Spring), a title determined by new ideals, the "Secessionists", during the turbulent years of their beginning, published a squareforma periodical that was bibliophilic in design and materials used. From its very beginnings, Ver Sacrum emphasized its leading role as the voice of an entirely new direction in graphic arts. Without Ver Sacrum, the development both of free fine-arts graphics and of applied graphic art in turn-of-the-century Vienna are inconceivable. In spite of being published in rather few copies only, the influence of this periodical reached far out into the remotest parts of the Danubian Monarchy, and magically drew young, up-and-coming artists of Vienna. For them, this city became just as much the center of spiritual orientation as for many of today's painters and writers from the Austrian provinces. Otto Wagner, as well as Hoffmann, Olbrich, and Loos became innovative pioneers of a new architecture. Schönberg, Berg, and Webern did the same for music where they, so to speak, took the place of Gustav Mahler, Richard Strauss, and Hugo Wolf. Meanwhile, the literary scene was shaped, dominated and determined by Arthur Schnitzler, Hugo von Hoffmannsthal, Peter Altenberg, Robert Musil, and Karl Kraus, who, by publishing the crusading periodical "Die Fackel" (The Torch), had become a veritable institution of the era, respected and feared both as a prosecutor and as an implacable and incorruptible critic. In the field of humanities, Egon Friedell ("Kulturgeschichte der Neuzeit") and Otto Weininger ("Geschlecht und Charakter") turned out to be the pilot thinkers of their age. Sigmund Freud discovered the netherworld of the unconscious and, as a result, evolved the therapeutic technique of psychoanalysis. His insights and theories, however, considerably transcended the narrow confines of psychiatry, or even medical science as such, ultimately attaining a much wider significance all over the world.

It ist not the purpose of this exhibition to provide a detailed over-all picture. Actually, "Secessionismus und die Graphischen Künste in Österreich 1900 — 1920" (Secessionism and Austrian Graphic Art 1900 — 1920) aims at giving the viewed characteristic insights into the turbulent early decades of Austrian cultural development in this century.

Comprising 77 exhibits, carefully selected from the approximately 6000 items in the Graphic Arts Collection of the Neue Galerie of the City of Linz (Wolfgang-Gurlitt-Museum), this medium-sized travelling exhibition will not only acquaint the visitor with the outstanding Austrian graphic artists in the era of Secessionism, but, in addition, will introduce him to quite a number of less-well-known, yet in many instances rather important and fascinating artists. To the open-minded and receptive observer, the vast range of the material on display this way provides a much more encompassing picture, which, at the same time, does justice to the variety and multiplicity of artistic trends and currents of the era. This has the added advantage of — at least implicitly — suggesting a bridge leading in the direction of the era between the two World Wars and to "Neue Sachlichkeit" (1918 to 1938).

The leading role of drawings as a seismograph of matters of the soul, and, at the same time, as a medium of the most direct, spontaneous, and personal artistic expression can be demonstrated not only through the material in our exhibition which, generally speaking, covers up to about the year 1920. Its continuity in Austrian fine arts of the 20th century ist chiefly underscored by the periods after 1945. In today's Austria, this dominant role tradition is being continued in autonomous contributions by highly significant artists like Arnulf Rainer, Walter Pichler, Josef Mikl, Hans Staudacher, Alfred Hrdlicka, Christian Ludwig Attersee, Günter Brus, and Othmar Zechyr. Added to this should be the names of artists of the youngest generation, among them Franz Blaas, Gunter Damisch, Herbert Brandl, and Karl-Heinz Klopf:

The current art scene in Austria is characterized both by pluralism of styles and an amazing density of creative effort. Within the context of international development, this scene logically presents a heterogenous image of artistic strivings, ranging from the classical media of painting, graphic arts, and sculpture, via object art and installations, all the way to video, respectively yet other, transcending media and methods.

The exhibit "Secessionism and Austrian Graphic Art 1900 to 1920" has been designed and compiled with the intention of complementing the rather narrow international definition of modern Austrian classics only with the highly pre-eminent names Klimt, Schiele, and Kokoschka (as well as Wagner, Hoffmann, and Loos, when it comes to architecture), and to undertake that type of documentation that aims at representing and conserving the broad, heterogenous spectrum of graphic arts in the waning years of the once great, multinational state. Artistic, intellectual, and spiritual life of Vienna, later, because of its excessive size, often jokingly called "hydrocephalus", benefited from the multitude of influences, mentalities, and talents which members of the vastly different races, peoples, and cultural spheres of the Monarchy contributed to the whole.

Vienna, the imperial capital and residence on the shores of the river Danube, in this era became the melting pot for mutually stimulating, interacting, and fertilizing seminal factors.

The characteristics of the situation of creative arts from 1900 to 1920 are not stylistic

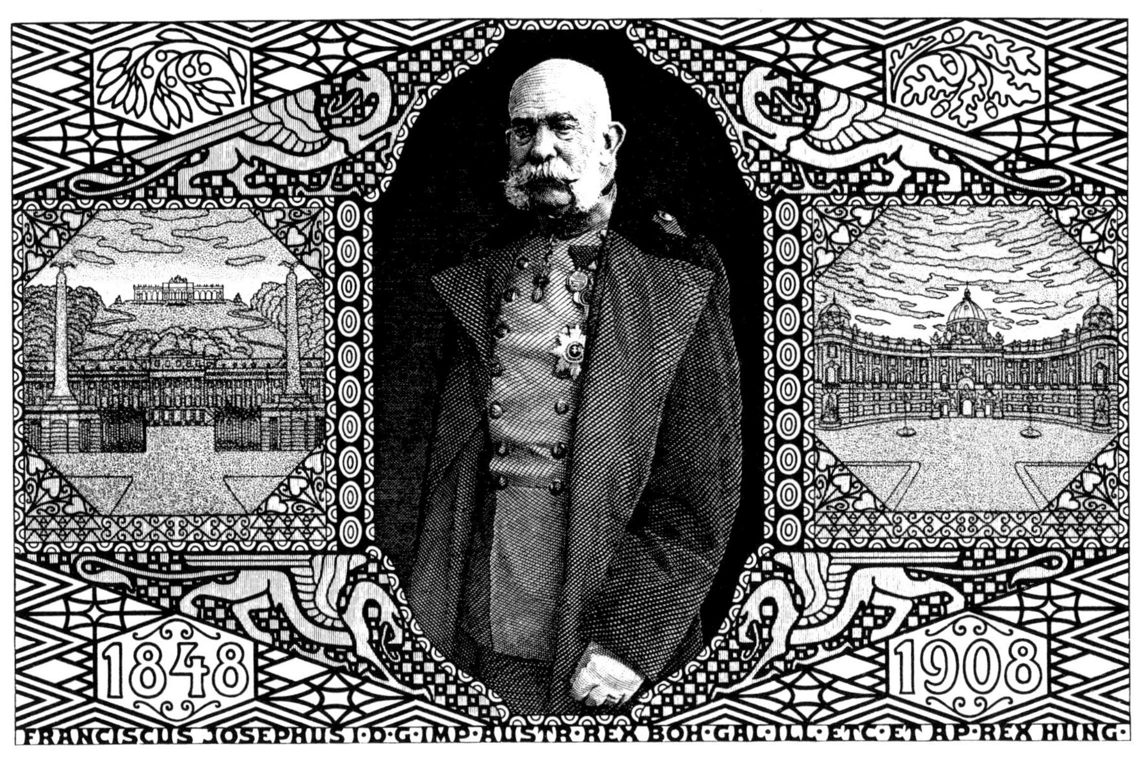

Postcard by Koloman Moser on the occasion of 60 anniversary of accession to the throne
by Emperor Franz Josef, 1908

and programmatic uniformity, but rather a significant variety and vitality born from contrasts and opposites opening up new vistas of understanding.

The fine arts Vienna cliché of a tranquil, harmonious fin-de-siècle era in our selection of works is shown expanded, and perhaps somewhat rectified, by adding names of artists, which, in many cases, even in Austria still have to be discovered to be given their proper valuation in art history. This applies to the Linz graphic artist Klemens Brosch (1894 to 1926), who ended his creative life much to soon by committing suicide at the age of 32, in a similar way as to Carl Anton Reichel (1874 — 1944), or to Franz von Zülow (1883 — 1963), whose work had been influenced, and eventually determined by the decorative color-area style of the Wiener Kunstgewerbeschule. Zülow was a master of convincing simplicity, the exponent of the clear, ornamentally rhythmizised black-and-white, which put its distinctive mark on many of his village scapes, scenarios, and landscapes painted between 1903 and 1920. The formal scope and possibilities of the medium of template prints (a technique somewhat akin to woodcut and block print), which Zülow used extensively in many of his works, can be discovered in comparable form with Jungnickel (Cat. Nos. 23/24). His animal representations, as for selection and use of media and techniques, can be compared with the much rarer woodcuts Bronica Koller-Pinell did in 1903 and 1904 (Cat. Nos. 38 to 40). In 1911, the Vienna graphic artist and painter Erwin Lang (1886 — 1962) published a portfolio of woodcuts dedicated to the interpretive dance of his then famous wife Grete Wiesenthal (Cat. Nos. 49/50). In these scenes, Lang reached, by consistent use of this black-and-white technique, a poster-like intensity of expression, leading the lineaments of Jugendstil over into the more emotionally based and more spontaneous idiom of expressionism. To him, stasis and exstasis are antipodes of a stylized concept not entirely free from pathos, exemplified a few years earlier in Oskar Kokoschka's "Träumende Knaben" (Dreaming Boys — Cat. Nos. 30 to 34) in a somewhat more narrative way, that probably stimulated Lang in this direction.

The art of the woodcut, a medium significantly renewed and revived by Munch and the German expressionists, for the Linz artist Egon Hofmann (1884 — 1972) was both the technique and form of expression he liked and used best. His landscapes and alpine rock formations (many of them dating back to World War I) show an affinity to comparable subjects dealt with by Hans Franta (1893 — 1983), who, even more than Hofmann himself, was influenced by his experiences in Siberia during that time. To these two perhaps should be added the Tyrolian landscape artist Alfons Walde, as well as the early expressionist artist Aloys Wach (1892 — 1940), who did mostly woodcuts and drawings. His early work, say, the small figural study of 1920 (Cat. No. 72), reminds one less of his acknowledged ideal Egger-Lienz than his middle and late land- and villagescapes, which appear reduced in merit by stereotyped repetition and his only too obvious willingness to adapt his style to that of his paragon.

The small-format graphic works (predominantly etchings, engravings and watercolors) by Felix Laske (Cat. Nos. 53 to 55) cultivate and endearing narrative style rich in detail. This underscores the lone-wolf status of this artist more than incidental stylistic or formal affinities to the work of some of his contemporaries.

Another essential "loner" of high degree — and one with a bizarre sense of humor to boot — was the writer and painter Fritz von Herzmanovsky-Orlando (1877 — 1954). His lyrically ironical, sensitive style of drawing has given us adventures and love scenes, spawned by a somewhat skewed and oddball imagination. They tend to evoke a wry smile in fellow Austrians because of their selfironical way of spoofing hierarchical bureaucracy, yet, for the very same reason, are seldom understood and appreciated beyond the confines of our small mountain republic.

Albert Paris von Gütersloh (1877 — 1973), too, was writer, poet, and artist at the same time. Only few of his lithographs show as clearly and impressively as the one from his 1924 thematic cycle "Cain and Abel" (Cat. No. 10) the balance of dream and reality so typical of Gütersloh's work.

The Carinthian expressionist Anton Kolig (1886 — 1950), in addition to a large number of important major paintings, left us mainly magnificent nudes charged with emotional tension. Since most of them date from years beyond the time scope of our exhibition, his work is here represented by an early woodcut (Cat. No. 41), presumably dating from 1905. He was obviously influenced by the Wiener Kunstgewerbeschule he had attended, and his work provides many points of comparison to that of artists and stylistic concepts referred to earlier in this text.

Works by Berthold Löffler, who taught at the germinal and stylistically highly influencial Wiener Kunstgewerbeschule, and by Emil Orlik, together with two unique drawings by the sensitive and sophisticated Graz artist Wilhelm Thöny (1888 — 1949) round out the selection shown in this exhibition. Thöny, by the way, spent the final years of his life — years that were particularly important in his creative work — in the USA: From 1938 to 1949 he lived and worked in New York City.

Stacho Gunia, born in Poland, and Franz Hofer, who, like Thöny, hailed from Graz and who, while studying at the Akademie der bildenden Künste in Vienna was a friend of Klemens Brosch from Linz, to this day are practically unknown even in Austria. In both cases, this results from a number of unfortunate factors. At least with Hofer, the fact that he was killed in action in World War I at the age of 38 may serve as a partial explanation. (Egon Schiele died at the age of 28, and Klemens Brosch, at that time severely addicted to morphine, committed suicide when he was only 32).

The social criticism that inspired some of the work of Carry Hauser (Cat. No. 12) tends to remind one of George Grosz, yet its cutting edge is different in an very personal, analytical way.

In Max Oppenheimer and his famous "Rosé Quartet" (Cat. No. 57) we find the symbiosis or synthesis of post-expressionist and post-cubist elements so characteristic for some of the artists of the period between the two World Wars.

The "visionary with the drawing pen" Alfred Kubin, in the sheets of his "Weber Portfolio" of 1903, left a profoundly moving documentary record of the soul, that speaks of early deep knowledge and prodigious psychic presentiment and foreboding. His startling parables of human bondage and entanglements are, next only to Schiele's later imagery, among the most exciting and impressive visual parallels to the psychoanalytical insights and delvings into the human soul of Sigmund Freud.

The eminence as a graphic artist of Gustav Klimt, who rightly has become the epitome of Vienna Secessionism, in this catalog has been fittingly delineated by Donald McClelland. We are proud to be able to provide for this important travelling exhibition to be shown in the USA three select and highly characteristic works from Klimt's rich graphic oeuvre that owes so much to the impulses of sketches.

The similarly precious unique water color by Egon Schiele (Cat. No. 64) marks the beginning of the process of a genius discovering and defining himself as an artist.

Within the Scant decade of high-strung, intense creativity, Schiele developed into an artist of singular status. If we see Klimt, so to speak, as the chronicler of aristocratic society and the atmosphere of the "grande bourgeoisie", then Schiele became the sensitive, compassionate, and uncompromising spokesman for the proletarian existence and for a startlingly new erotic reality.

His early engagement for the cause of man, quite on the same level as that of the early Kokoschka around 1910 to 1915, unvarnished and of self-tormenting honesty, helped to expose the problems and the grimy side of an waning great era in Austrian art und intellectual history, an era that had been rich in startling insights and major break-throughs.

The Neue Galerie of the City of Linz/Wolfgang Gurlitt Museum is happy to present the exhibition "Secessionism and Austrian Graphic Art 1900 — 1920" to an alert and receptive public in the United States of America. In this vein, the gratitude of the undersigned as well as a message of greeting from the Mayor of the Upper Austrian capital Linz, Dr. Franz Dobusch, go to the Smithsonian Institution's Traveling Exhibition Service, first and foremost to its Director Anna R. Kohn, as well as to Mr. Donald McClelland, who for several years has put much time and effort into furthering and promoting this "joint venture". Beyond this, he contributed a knowledgable and sensitive article for this catalogue, for which he certainly deserves added thanks.

At this point I also should like to thank all the directors, curators, and their colleagues involved in this effort at the American museums, galleries, and universities at which this exhibition will be on display for their interest and effort in assuring a truly professional presentation of the material.

Thanks of the Neue Galerie der Stadt Linz go in particular to the sponsors of the exhibition, as well as to all the people both in the USA and in Austria who have helped to make this exhibition materialize.

Specifically, they are

H. E. Ambassador Dr. Friedrich Hoess, and
Counselor Dr. Ferdinand Trauttmansdorff;
both at the Austrian Embassy in Washington, D.C.

Dr. Wolfgang Waldner, Director of the Austrian Cultural Institute, New York

Mr. Reinhard Göweil of the Chemie Holding AG, Linz, Austria

Austrian Airlines (AUA), Vienna and New York

Dr. Johann Marte of the Austrian Federal Ministry of Science und Research

In concluding, I should also like to thank my colleagues in the museum of which I am the director: Dr. Elisabeth Thaller, Ms. Ulrike Fanta, Ms. Edith Füreder, Mr. Albert Friedl, Mr. Franz Rechberger, Mr. Josef Reindl, Mr. G. Laher, and Mr. Viktor Bucher. All of them have given their best in assisting me in the rather lengthy and involved preparatory work for the catalogue, the exhibition itself, and in matters of transportation.

Peter Baum

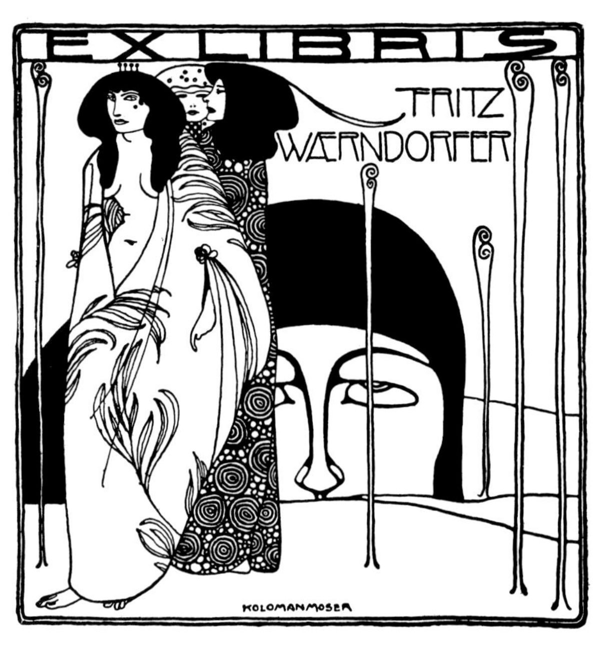

Koloman Moser: Ex Libris for Fritz Wärndorfer, 1903

Art and chemistry are closely related fields. Innovation and creativity have the same main springs. As a result it is rather logical for *Agrolinz* and *Chemie Linz,* as part of the Austrian Industries AG, to become sponsors of the Fine Arts. By promoting modern art in our country we have committed ourselves to a task somewhat akin to our development as an enterprise.
A continual learning process and confronting the new and unknown are part of our lives.
We wish visitors to this exhibition a stimulating encounter with Austrian Art and hope they will like it.

Artists・Catalogue

24

Klemens Brosch

Albin Egger-Lienz

Hans Franta

Stascho Cunia

Albert Paris Gütersloh

Carry Hauser

Fritz v. Herzmanovsky-Orlando

Franz Hofer

Egon Hofmann

Ludwig Heinrich Jungnickel

Gustav Klimt

Oskar Kokoschka

Broncia Koller-Pinell

Anton Kolig

Alfred Kubin

Erwin Lang

Oskar Laske

Berthold Löffler

Max Oppenheimer

Emil Orlik

Carl Anton Reichel

Egon Schiele

Wilhelm Thöny

Aloys Wach

Alfons Walde

Franz von Zülow

Klemens Brosch

Born Linz, 21. 10. 1894
died Linz, 17. 12. 1926
Son of a school principal who was a local historian.
One of the most important rediscovered artists of
Austrian art from the early twentieth century. Like
E. Schiele and R. Gerstl he died young. Psychically
crushed by the impact of World War One atrocities in
Galicia and the personal hardships, he committed
suicide in the Pöstlingberg cemetary.
1908—10 attended Eisenbahnakademie (Railway
Academy) and then the Realschule; graduation in
1913. His teachers noticed his unusual draftsmanship
and ambition. The sixteen-year-old returned from his
summer vacation with more than 1000 drawings and
sketches.
Most important for this budding talent was his precise
and persistent drawing from nature. Landscape and
objects were motifs for exact observation. His
intention was to capture their essence and to confront
them with human experiential and perceptual modes.
Despite certain influences by symbolists, Klinger and
Thoma, the Secessionists and Japanese woodcut,
Brosch developed an unique and intense drawing
style, which was a synthesis of above sources and the
outcome of his personal suffering and sensibility.
Brosch was a "radiologist of reality and truth" who —
similar to A. Kubin — exposed the abyss of the human
psyche.
In 1913 Brosch and other artists founded the art
association "MAERZ" in Linz, which is the leading
club of Upper Austrian painters, sculptors and graphic artists to this day. In 1913 he also enrolled for a
brief time at the Vienna Akademie der bildenden Künste (fine arts, class Rudolf Bacher). 1914 volunteer in
Galicia; took opium to deal with the impact of the
atrocities there. 1915 return to Linz as a sick man;
exhibited 115 works about the war, which were highly
praised. 1915/16 continued his studies with Ferdinand
Schmutzer in Vienna and received highest honors.
1919 sketches for token money of Upper Austrian
town-ships; his designs rate among the highest of this
small-format genre. Repeated stays in mental clinics
did not relieve Brosch's drug addiction.
After decades of almost total neglect, retrospective
exhibitions in several Austrian provincial capitals after
1979 placed his oeuvre, primarily in Linz collections,
within a larger art historical context.

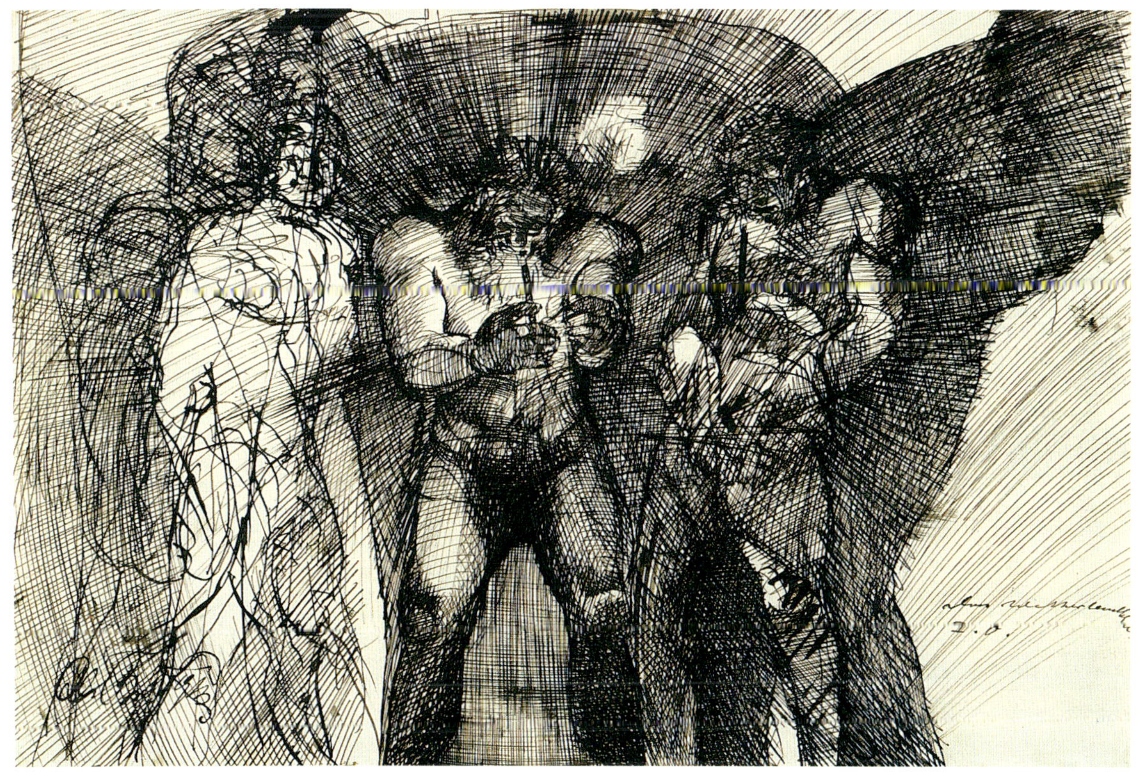

Cat.   1

1
Klemens Brosch
Storm Brewing, 1913
pen and ink on paper, 21 x 31 cm
Inv.Nr. 3247

2
Klemens Brosch
View from the Window, 1913
pencil on cardboard, 33,5 x 25 cm
Inv.Nr. 5054

3
Klemens Brosch
Train Station, 1926
watercolor, 30,5 x 87 cm
Inv.Nr. 3253

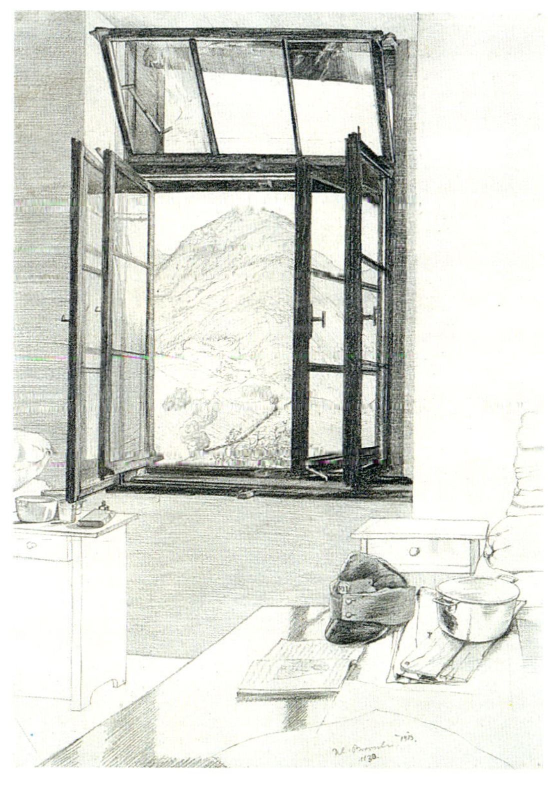

Cat.   2

28

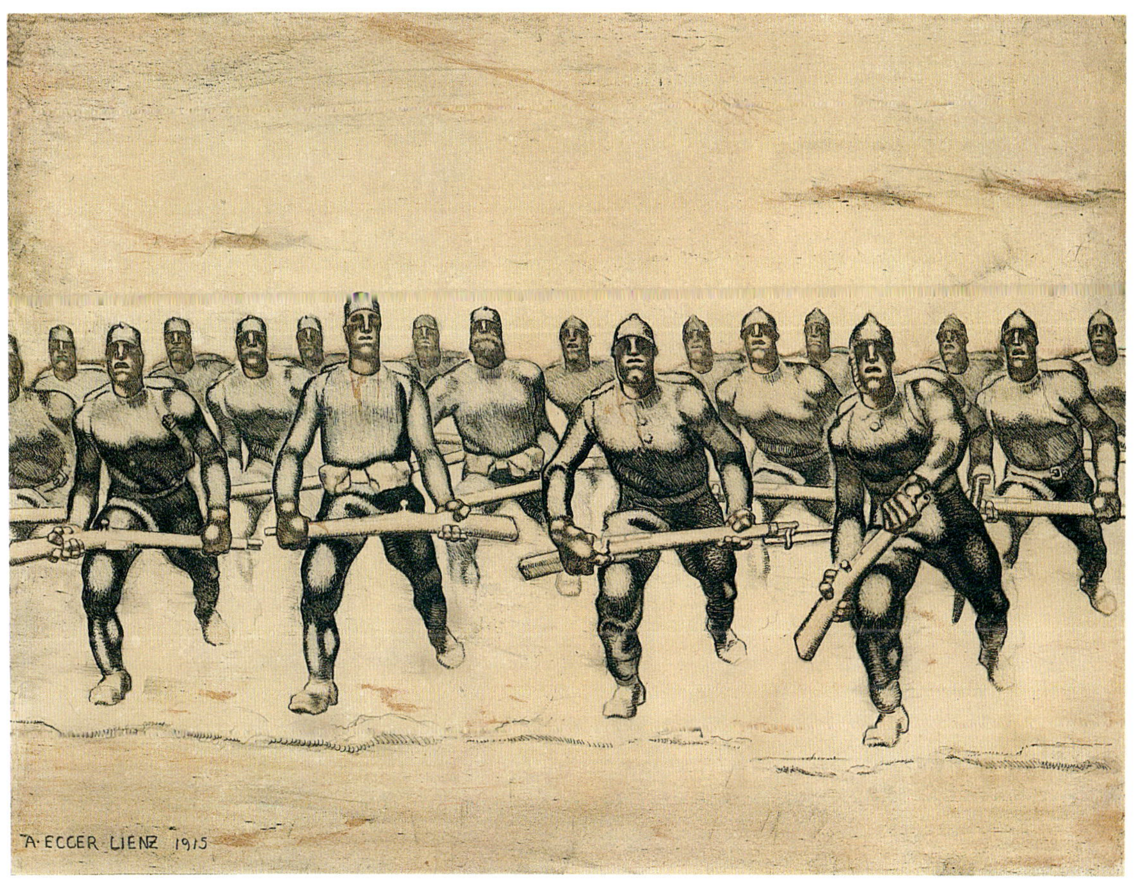

Cat. 4

Albin Egger-Lienz

born Striebach bei Lienz, East Tyrol, 1868
died Rautsch near Bolzano, 1926
First instruction from his father who was a church painter. 1884—93 studied at the Academy in Munich. Until his move to Vienna in 1899, he had a studio in Munich. 1911/12 taught at the Hochschule für bildende Kunst (fine arts) in Weimar. Then he settled in South Tyrol.
Albin Egger-Lienz began painting in a naturalistic style. Later he concentrated on specific narrative motifs. Early in his career, he chose rural life as his main topic, which he increasingly monumentalized at the turn of the century. His confrontation with the works of Ferdinand Hodler led to simple and symbolic representations. World War One, which he experienced first as soldier, then (1916) as a war painter, left an indelible mark on his personal and artistic developement. Works of this period portray the lunacy of warfare and have remained monumental documents of and memorials against war to this day.

In his fifties he still strove imperturbed after forms of artistic expression; for this reason he declined a teaching position in 1918 at the Vienna Academy. He abandoned the linear style of his mature period and returned to the picturesque naturalism of his early work without jettisoning the achievements of his monumental period. Therefore he arrived at a new synthesis in the twenties: The free flow of his early period combined with more vivid colors; colors flow together and are no longer clear and hard.
While his early paintings were symbols of heavy, strenuous activity, the later ones are rather passive, contemplative, and tranquil. Albin Egger-Lienz left a complex oeuvre, unique in its expressiveness and monumentality, timeless in its political message.

4

Albin Egger-Lienz
1915, 1915
lithograph, 72 x 90,5 cm
Inv. Nr. 3346

Hans Franta

Born Linz, 1893
died Linz, 1983
His oeuvre comprises about 2000 pastels, about
1000 oil paintings, several hundred water-colors,
drawings and prints. 1913—21 his most creative
years. Attended the Akademie der bildenden Künste
(fine arts) in Vienna for a couple of months, followed
by military service and Russian captivity. Essentially a
self-taught artist. The work of his early period is
unencumbered by speculation, compelling in its
simplicity. Franta studied nature as it related to man
and his psychic sensitivity. This applies above all to
the small-format graphic art which is simple and
ambiguous as well as realistic and mysterious. His
experience with Russian poetry and melancholy were
also a source of inspiration in his later work which
does not match his early production. In his early
career Franta used the possibilities of abstraction. To
describe the elementary character of a landscape, a
wooden hut, several fields or a group of snow-capped
houses he reduced his pictorial language to a few
dominant and sometimes simple compositional
elements. For the artist, the tone of the paper was
often as important as the colors or the graphic tools.
1913 Matura, participated in the exhibition of the
Oberösterreichischer Kunstverein (Upper Austrain Art
Club). 1914 studied art history at the University of
Vienna. Volunteered in World War One on the Russian
front; captured in the same year. 1921 he was
transferred as a medical patient via Moscow, Kiev,
Kharkov to Tomsk in Siberia. Married a Russian, met
David Burljuk, a member of the "Blauer Reiter". 1921
return to Linz. 1925—29 studied at the Akademie der
bildenden Künste (fine arts) in Vienna. Until 1957
teaching jobs in secondary schools in Linz. 1976 large
retrospective exhibition in the Neue Galerie der Stadt
Linz emphasizing his early period as well as the
equally important pastels of his last years.

5

Hans Franta
Toolshed in the Snow, 1916
pencil, tempera, white wash on tinted paper,
23,7 x 32,1 cm
Inv.Nr. 2648

6

Hans Franta
Harbor with Ships, about 1916
aquarelle, 21,5 x 26,2 cm
Inv.Nr. 2650

7

Hans Franta
Tomsk, 1918
ink and aquarelle on paper, 23,7 x 32,1 cm
Inv.Nr. 2649

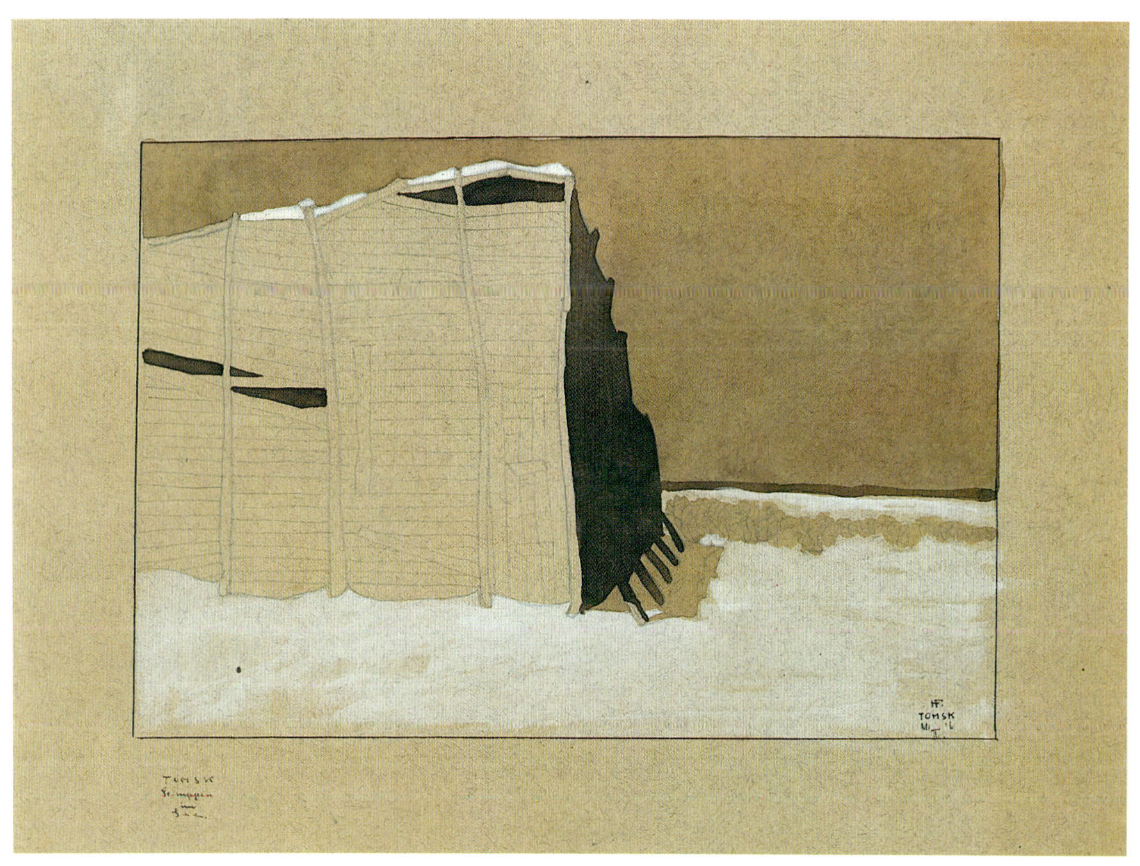

Cat. 5

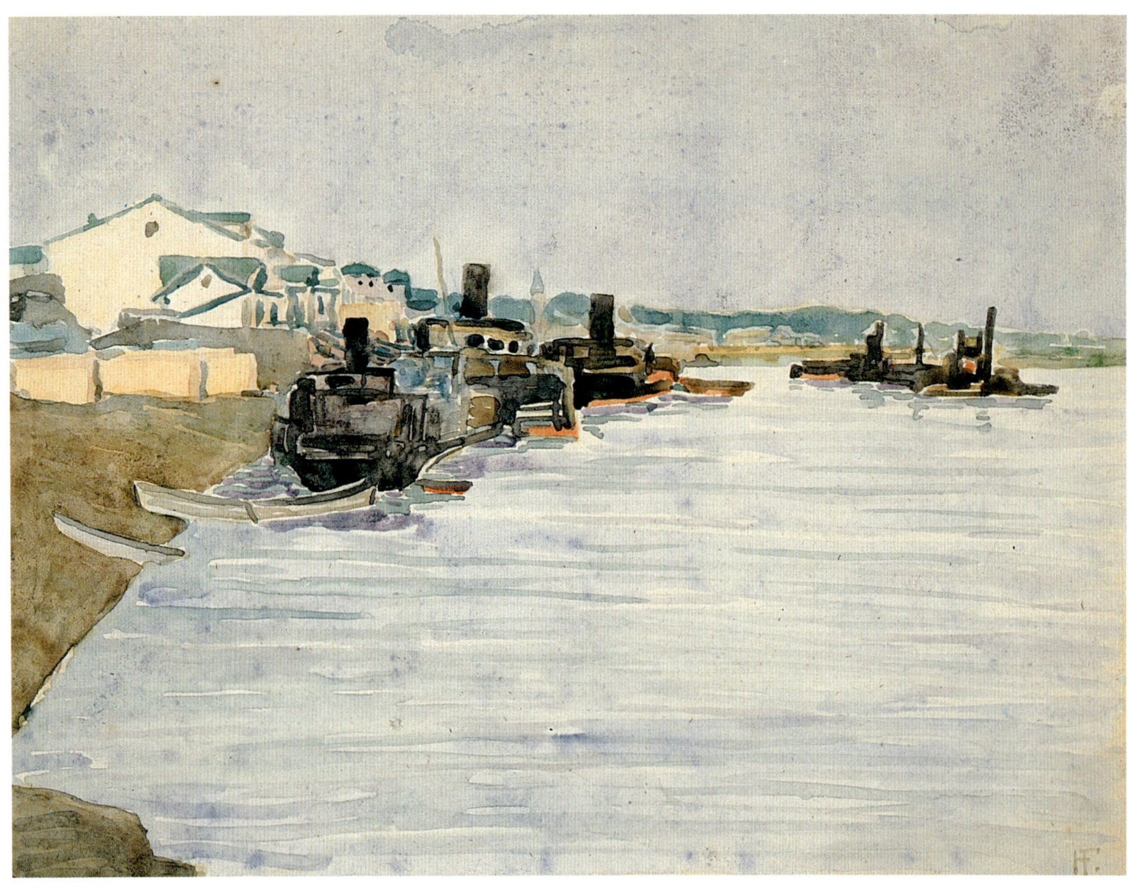

Cat. 6

32

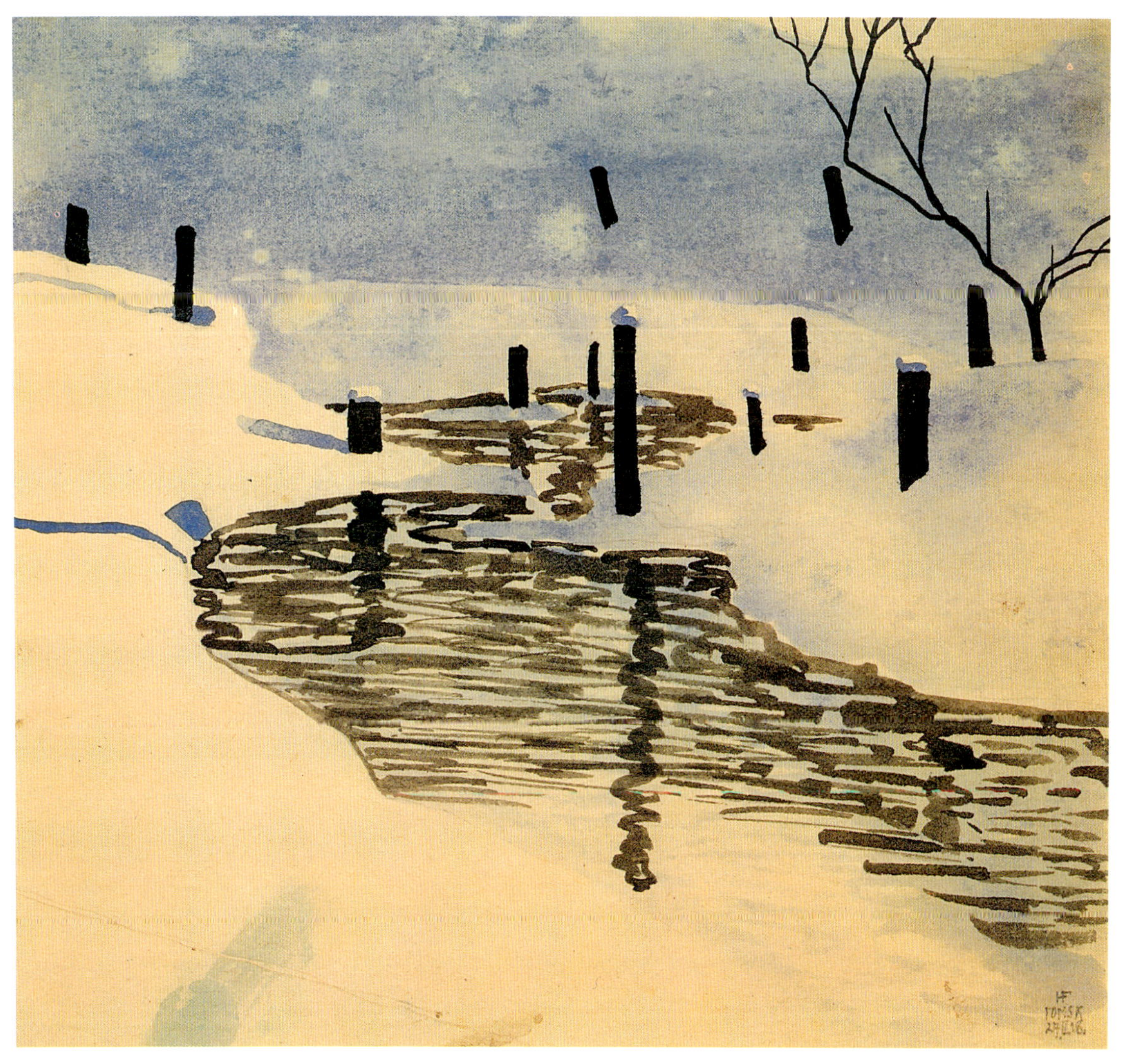

Cat. 7

Stascho Gunia

Born on July 26, 1897, in Przemysl, now Poland; died on August 8, 1966 in Vienna, where he worked probably since 1920/25.
Only in recent times Stacho Gunia has been rediscovered as a highly original artist of the period between the two World Wars. As we know from paintings that have re-surfaced recently, he seems to have been influenced — at least in part — by Egon Schiele.
It is likely that in his day Gunia remained virtually unknown in the world of galleries and art dealers, since practically no other facts or data about his life have become available.

8

Stascho Gunia
Dead Monk, 1924
colored drypoint, 18/20, 17,7 x 20 cm
Inv.Nr. 3726

9

Stascho Gunia
**Portrait of a Man with Orchid
(Self Portrait), ca. 1925**
pencil and colored pencil on tissue paper,
36 x 28,7 cm
Inv.Nr. 3727

Cat. 8

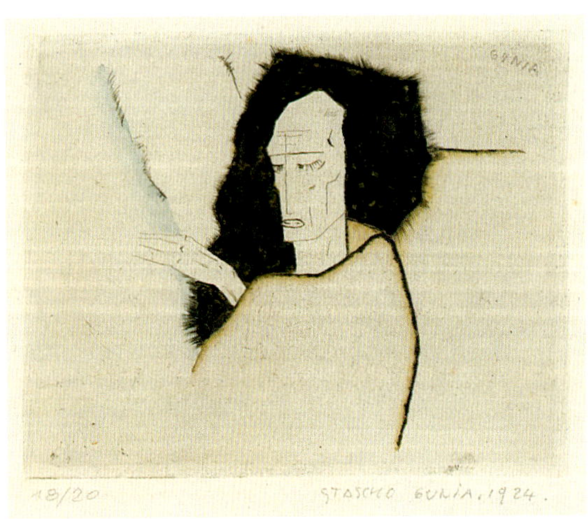

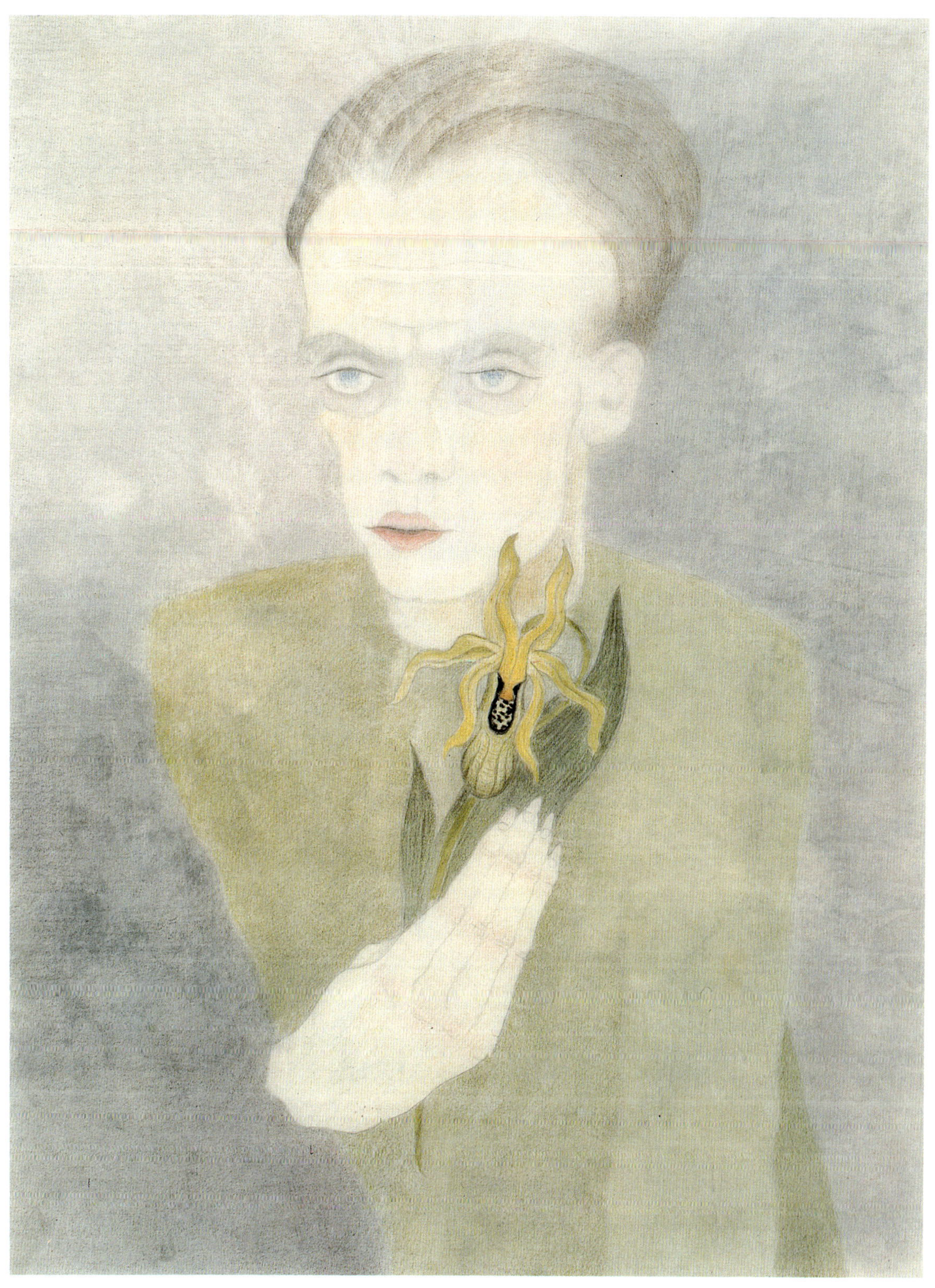

Albert Paris Gütersloh

Born Vienna, 1887
died Baden bei Wien, 1973
Training as actor, performed primarily in Germany, for instance with Max Reinhardt at the Deutsches Theater, Berlin. 1909 terminated his stage career due to ill health; first exhibition of paintings with the "Neukunstgruppe". Many more exhibitions until the outbreak of World War One. Concurrently active as writer, contacts with Robert Musil, Franz Blei, Hugo von Hofmannsthal, and Hermann Bahr. 1919/21 travel to Munich, Berlin, Paris. 1928/30 in Cagnes-sur-Mer. Return to Vienna. 1929—38 Professor at the Wiener Kunstgewerbeschule (applied arts). 1938 dismissed by the Nazis. 1940 ban as "degenerate artist". 1947 founder of the Art Club, its long-term president. Members of this Club determined and influenced decisively the artistic life of the Second Austrian Republic. Important pioneer of the "Wiener Schule des phantastischen Realismus" (Viennese School of Fantastic Realism). One of the most versatile personalities of Viennese intellectual life. Gütersloh was a painter, water-colorist, illustrator, writer, teacher, organizer, pioneer, and critical contemporary. Albert Paris Gütersloh's beginnings as an artist are associated with G. Klimt and his circle. Soon he developed his own graphic style of crystalline forms which approached the surrealists. 1911—13 lived in Paris and was a student of Maurice Denis who considered color as the central compositional element on a canvas. Thus his pre-war oeuvre displays great variety. After the war, in the mid-twenties, Gütersloh simplified and standardized the forms of his objects, and possibly influenced by the Neue Sachlichkeit and the Magic Realism, put more emphasis on realism without fully renouncing the surrealist elements of his style.

10
Albert Paris Gütersloh
from Cain and Abel, 1924
lithograph, 45,7 x 33,4 cm
Inv.Nr. 2778

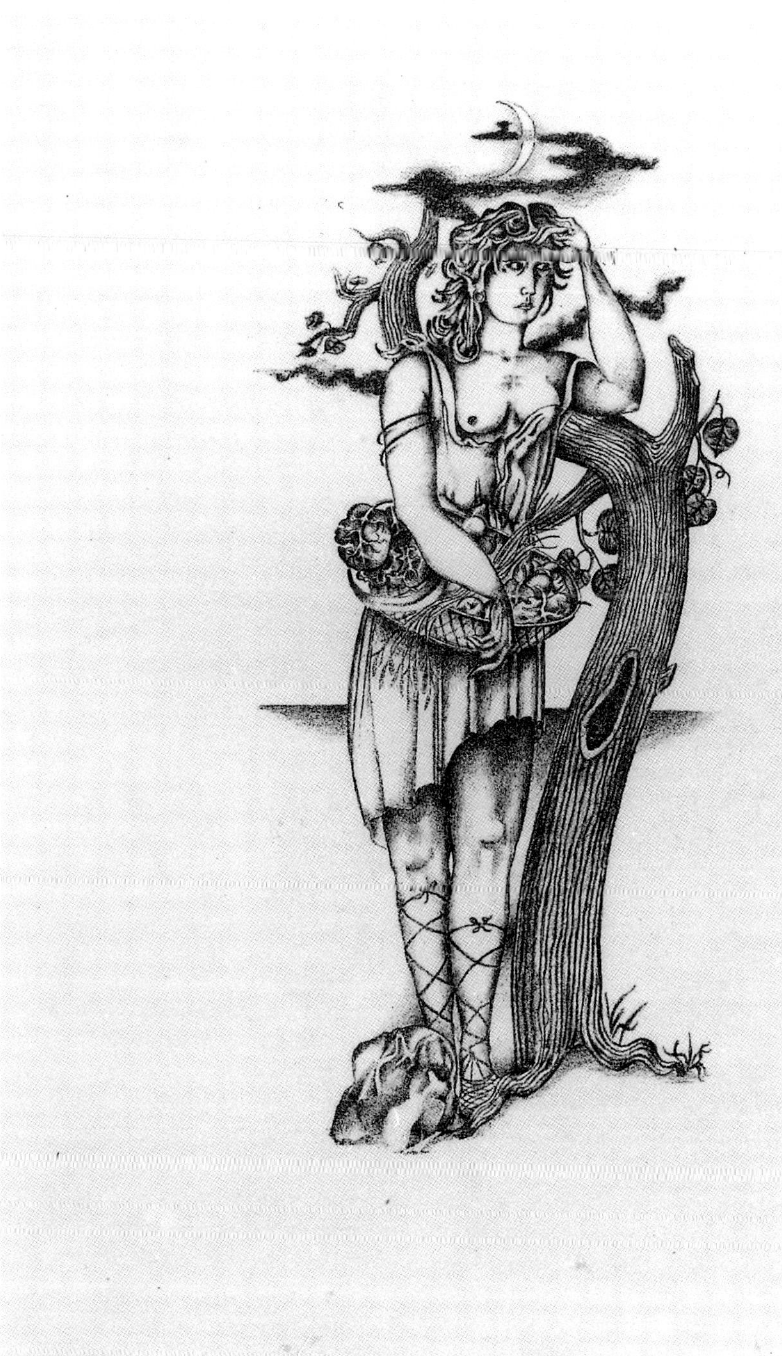

Cat. 10

Carry Hauser

Born on February 16, 1895, in Vienna. Died in October, 28, 1985, in Rekawinkel, Lower Austria.

(Carl Maria) Hauser started his education in fine arts at the "Graphische Lehr- und Versuchsanstalt", continuing in the old "Kunstgewerbeschule" in Vienna, where he was tutored by Oskar Strnad and Anton von Kenner. Starting in 1914, he participated in World War I. After the war had ended in 1918, he worked as a free-lance artist. Thematically, his oeuvre is dedicated to man torn between fear and temptation, but to representation of religious themes as well. Some of his early drawings and paintings are reminiscent of the works of Georg Grosz, while in the woodblock sequence "Book of Dreams" Hauser did in 1921, he employed the stylistic "vocabulary" of expressionism. But soon thereafter, in his paintings he displayed a clearly delineated, very personal style, placing him somewhere between cubism and the Vienna School of Magic Realism ("Nocturnal Wanderer", 1920).

In the thirties, Hauser also worked as a stage designer, e.g. at the Vienna Burgtheater, designing the sets for a play by his friend Franz Theodor Csokor. But all of this did not suffice for his boundless creative energy: he began writing as well. Among his major literary works were "Eine Geschichte vom verlorenen Sohn" (A Story of the Lost Son), "Maler, Tod und Frau" (Painter, Death and Woman), as well as a book titled "Von Kunst und Künstlern in Österreich" (Of Art and Artists in Austria) which he himself illustrated and which was published in 1937, and a Book of Cities he himself had illustrated.

From 1925 to 1938, Carry Hauser was a member of the influential "Hagenbund", serving as its president from 1928 onward.

In 1939, Carry Hauser was in the process of emigrating to Australia, when he was caught short in Switzerland by the outbreak of World War II. There, as most other refugees, he was denied a work permit.

Having returned to Vienna in 1947, he continued to draw and paint, yet now using al large-area style of great intensity of color. As for themes, man, more then ever, was now the focus of Hauser's work — man in his tragic isolation and in his being determined by unfathomable fate. ("The Prophet", 1950; "To the Mothers of the Atomic Age", 1965.)

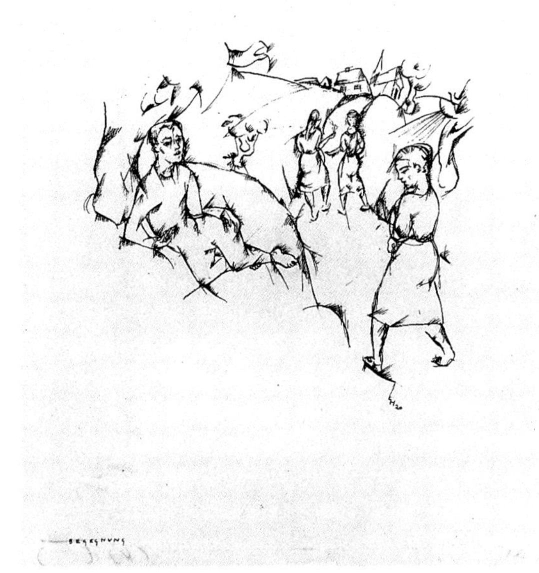

Cat. 11

11

Carry Hauser
The Meeting, 1920
pen and ink on paper, 27,4 x 22,3 cm
Inv.Nr. 4418

12

Carry Hauser
The Doctors, 1921
pen and ink, 43 x 31,8 cm
donation by Norli and Hellmut Czerny
Inv.Nr. 3373

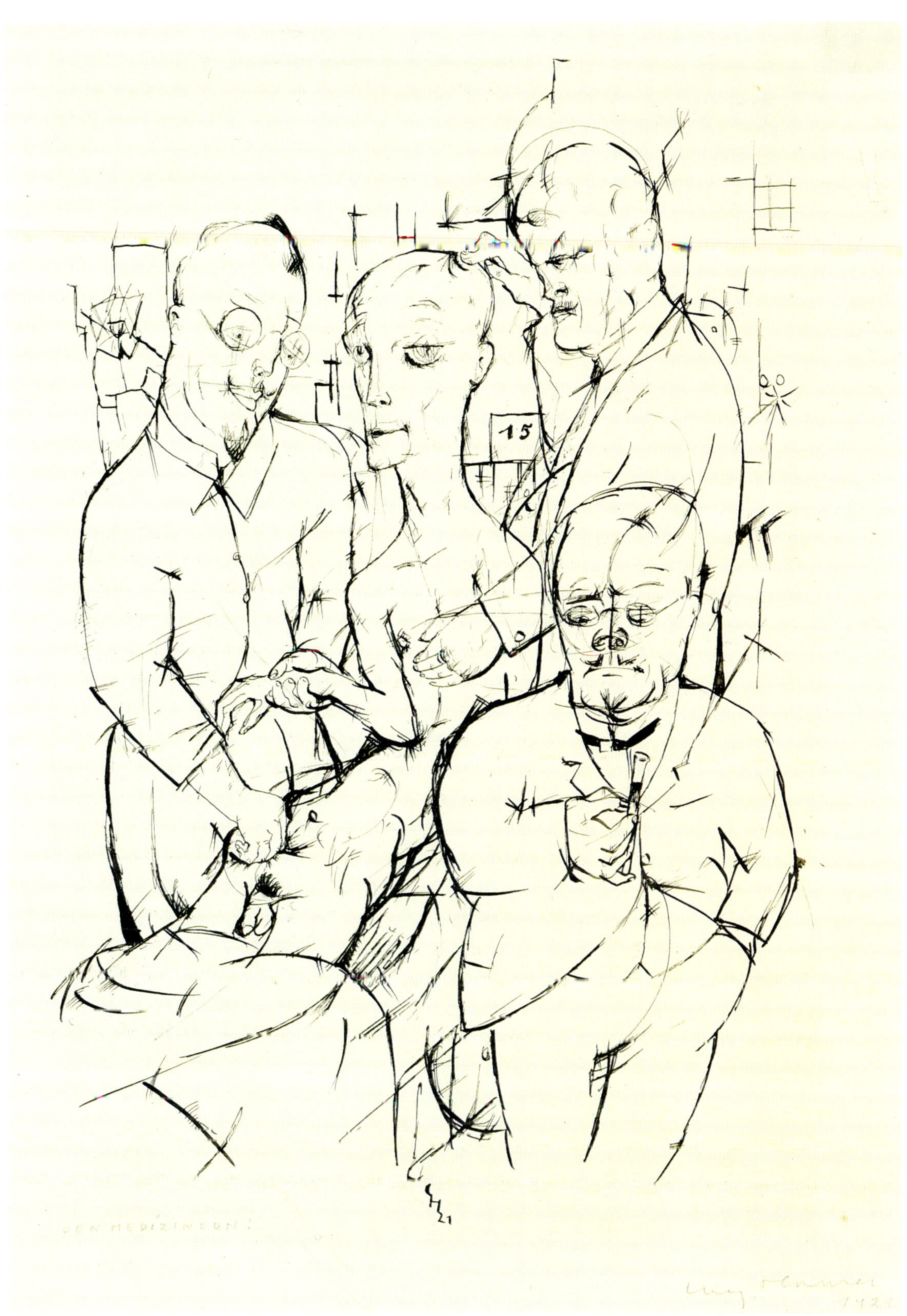

Fritz v. Herzmanovsky-Orlando

Born on April 30, 1877 in Vienna, the only child of Sektionschef (highest civil-service grade in the old Austro-Hungarian Monarchy) Dr. Emil Ritter von Herzmanovsky-Orlando, he was baptized in Vienna's venerable "Karlskirche". The artist's ancestors on the paternal side had been top-ranking civil servants, officials, and officers, while on his mother's side, the lineage leads back to Florence, Venice and Byzantium (Constantinople).

1887—1906	Fritz von Herzmanovsky-Orlando attended the prestigious "Theresianum" in Vienna, at that time a highschool with a clearly upper-class student body.
1896—1903	He studied architecture at "Technische Hochschule" (College of Engineering and Technology) in Vienna, graduating as "Stadtbaumeister" (something combining the qualifications of an architect and of a municipal contractor). In this period, a close friendship to the painter, graphic artist, and writer Alfred Kubin developed.
1908	He became a member of the "Zentralkommission für Kunst und historische Denkmalpflege" (Central Commission for Fine Arts and Care of Historical Monuments.)
Starting 1903	he worked as an architect, mainly on restauration projects in Vienna, Lower Austria, and Tyrol. Some of this work was commissioned by the then pretender to the Habsburg throne Franz Ferdinand. In this period, he also journeyed to England and the Netherlands. After his marriage in 1911 he went on numerous journeys to Egypt, Greece, and the Greco-Venecian Isles.
1914	He ceased his professional career for reasons of health and moved to Meran, then still within the Austro-Hungarian Monarchy.
1939—1946	For this period in his life, World War II caused Fritz Herzmanovsky-Orlando to move to Malcesine on Lake Garda in Italy.
1946	Return to Meran.
1954	On May 17, Fritz von Herzmanovsky-Orlando, aged 77, died on Rametz Castle in Meran, South Tyrol, Italy.

13

Fritz von Herzmanovsky-Orlando
Zoology, 1919
pencil on paper, 20 x 25 cm
Inv.Nr. 2084

14

Fritz von Herzmanovsky-Orlando
Pharmacy in the Succession States, 1919
aquarelle and pencil on paper, 28 x 23 cm
Inv.Nr. 2082

15

Fritz von Herzmanovsky-Orlando
Österreich Mostindien, 1919
colored pencil, 20 x 25 cm
Inv.Nr. 2102

16

Fritz von Herzmanovsky-Orlando
The Spirit of Birds Petitions Diana, 1919
colored pencil on paper, 20 x 25 cm
Inv.Nr. 2103

17

Fritz von Herzmanovsky-Orlando
Gallants in the Fortress, 1919
pencil, 20 x 25 cm
Inv.Nr. 2107

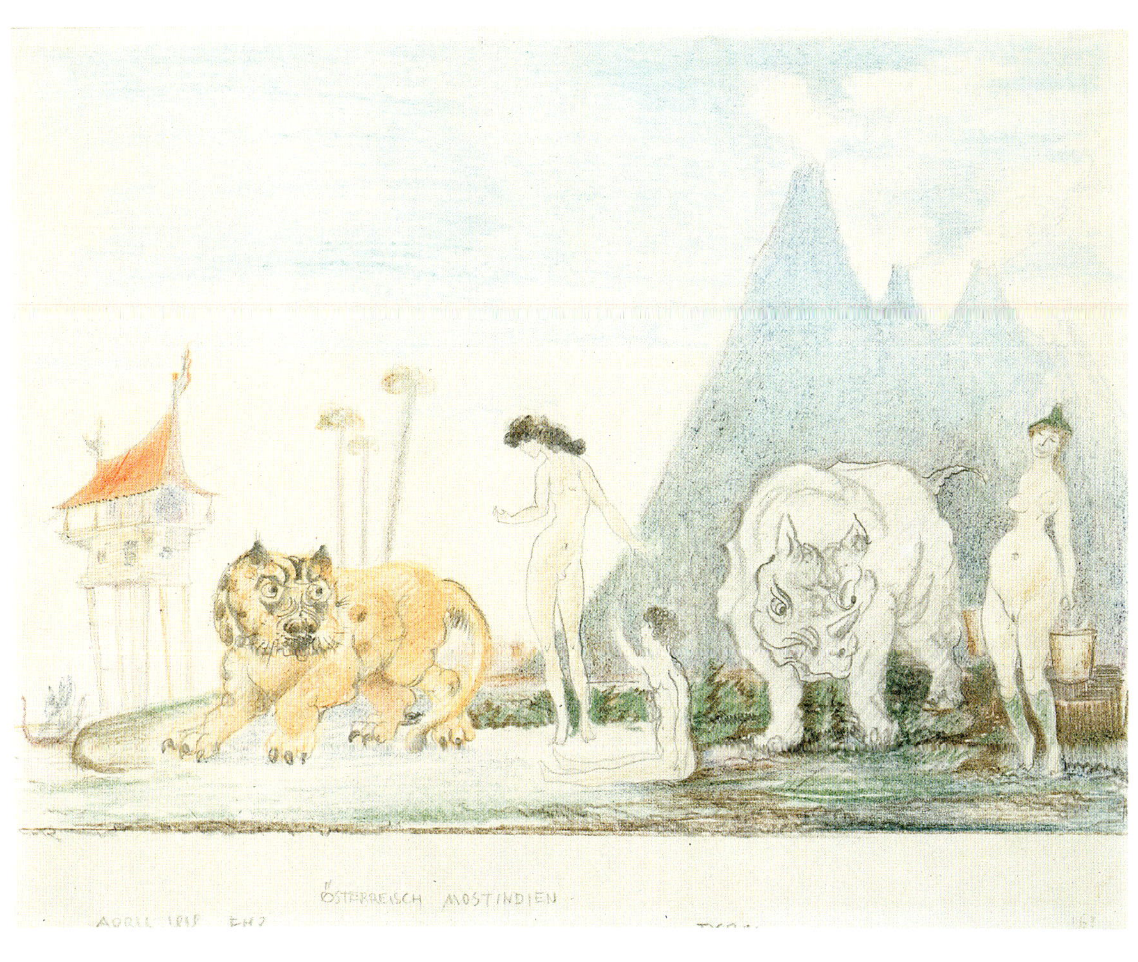

Cat. 15

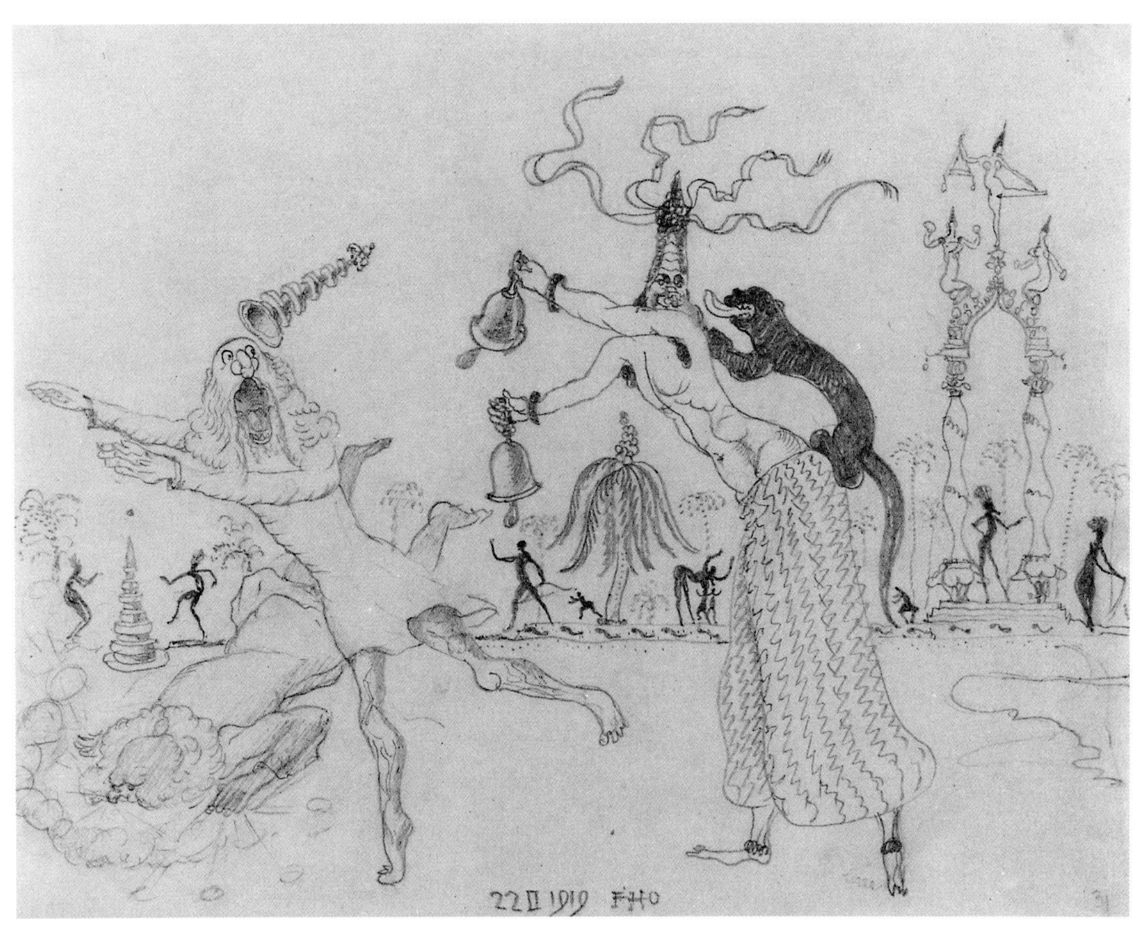

Cat. 13

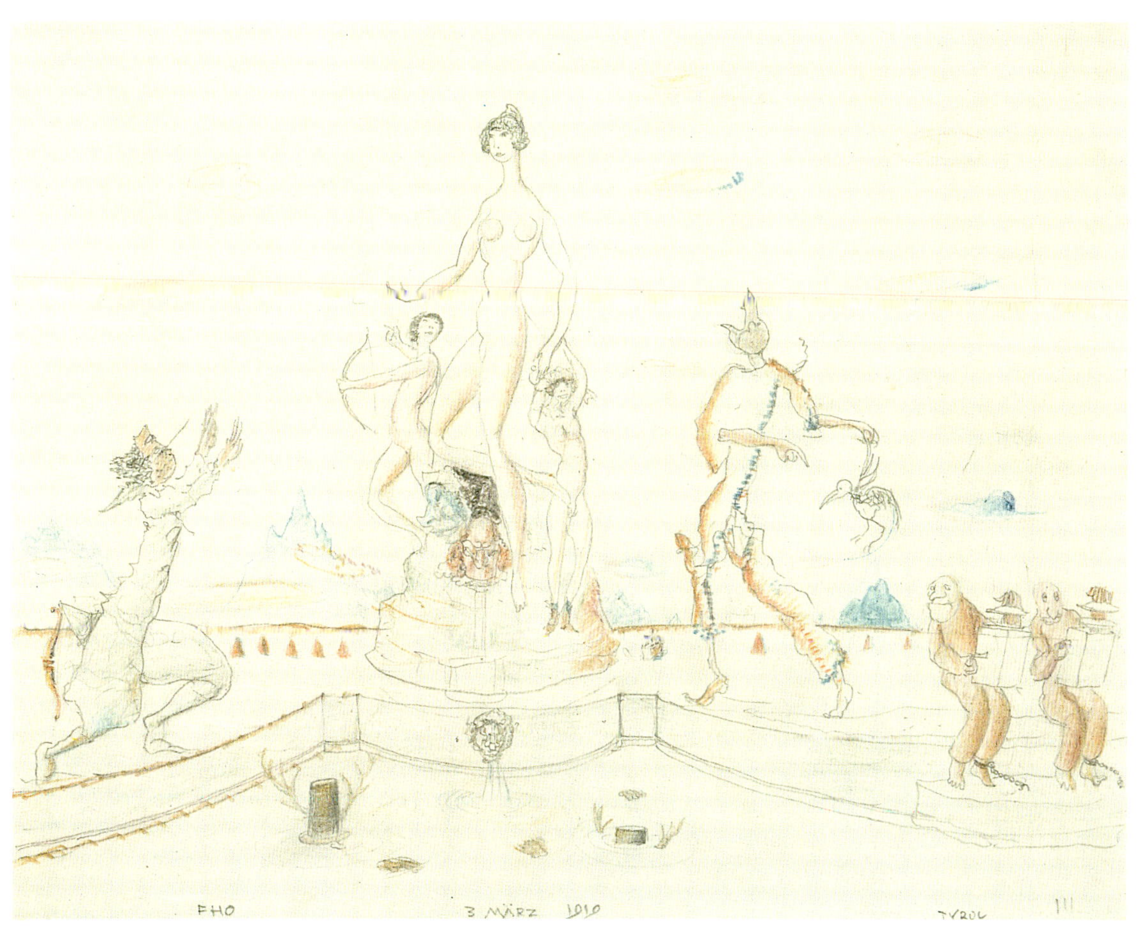

Cat. 16

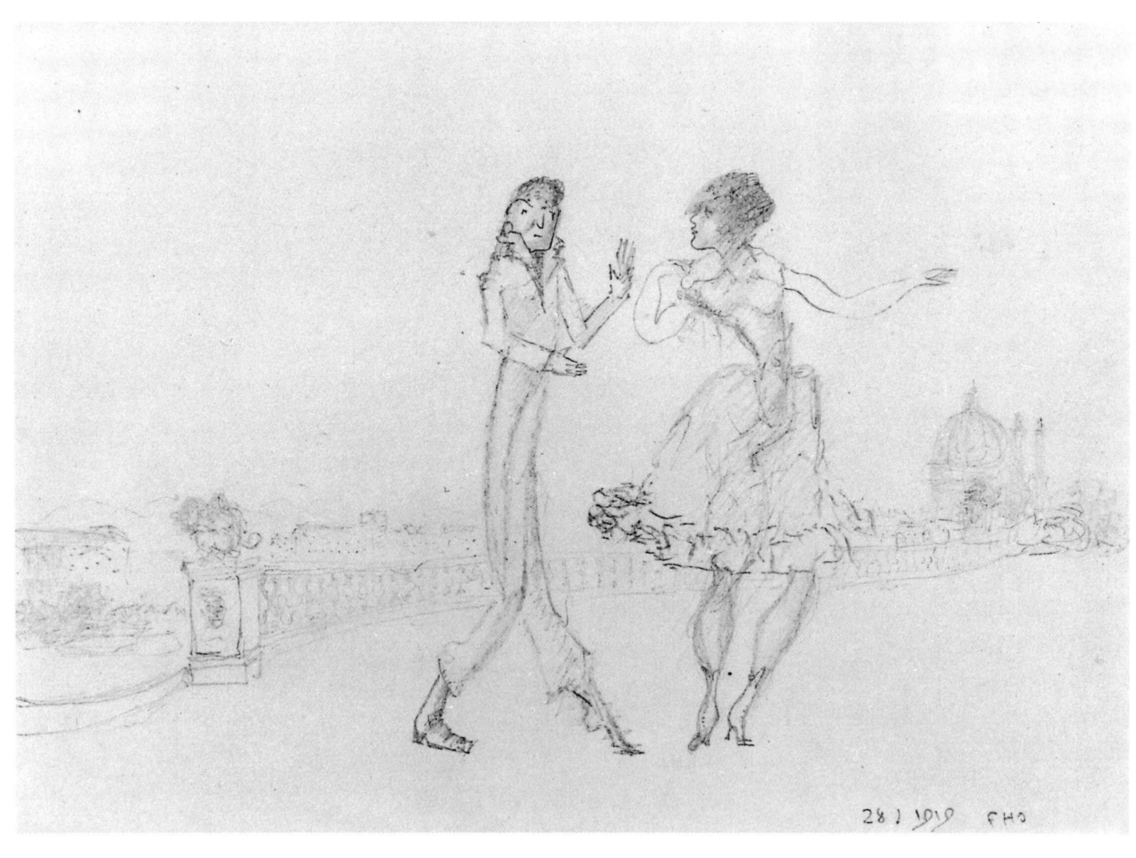

Cat. 17

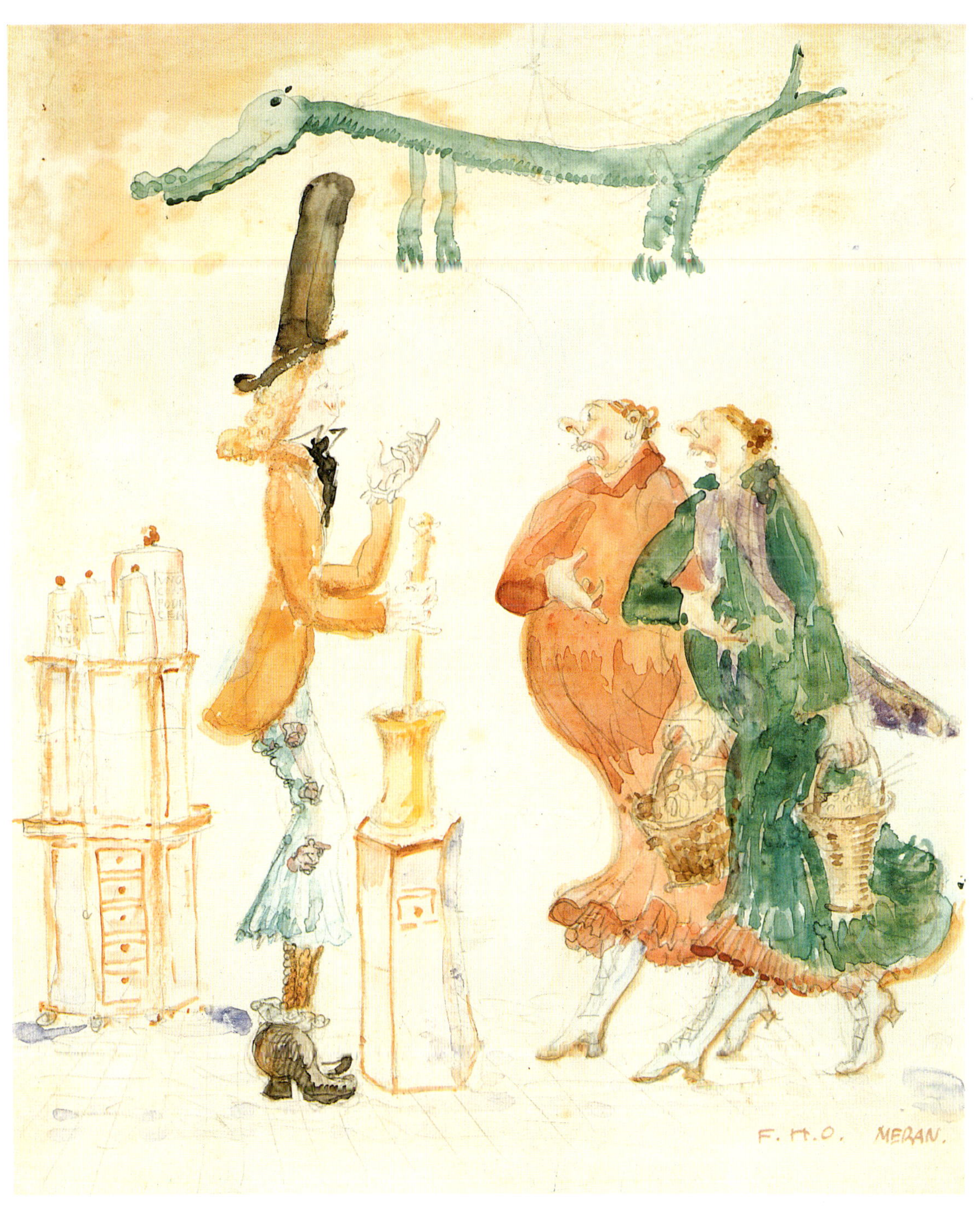

Cat. 14

Franz Hofer

Born on December 24, 1885, in Graz, Styria, Austria. Killed in action during World War I somewhere in Galicia on May 3, 1915. First, he studied lithography in his home town, then, still as a youngster, became footloose, travelling more or less at random. During this period, he spent a few months at the Dresden Academy of fine arts, attending practice sessions and the evening drawing classes. Subsequently, Franz Hofer worked for three years in Graz as a student of Alfred von Schrötter. In 1909, he started attending classes at the Academy of Creative Arts, working in the classes of Delug and Schmutzer (Print media). In 1914, his etching "Descent from the Cross" earned him a scholarship to go to Russia. However, the outbreak of World War I kept him from taking advantage of this opportunity.

18

Franz Hofer
Laborers on a Scaffolding, ca. 1910
drawing ink on tinted paper, 21 x 21 cm
Inv.Nr. 2779

19

Franz Hofer
Bridge Building, ca. 1910
drawing ink on Tinted paper, 24 x 20,6 cm
Inv.Nr. 2780

Cat. 18

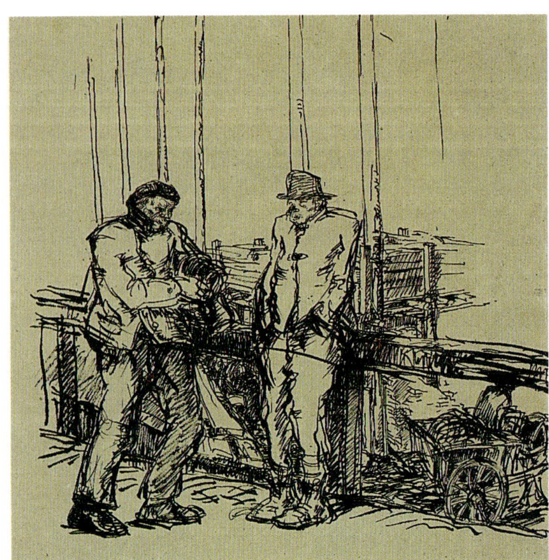

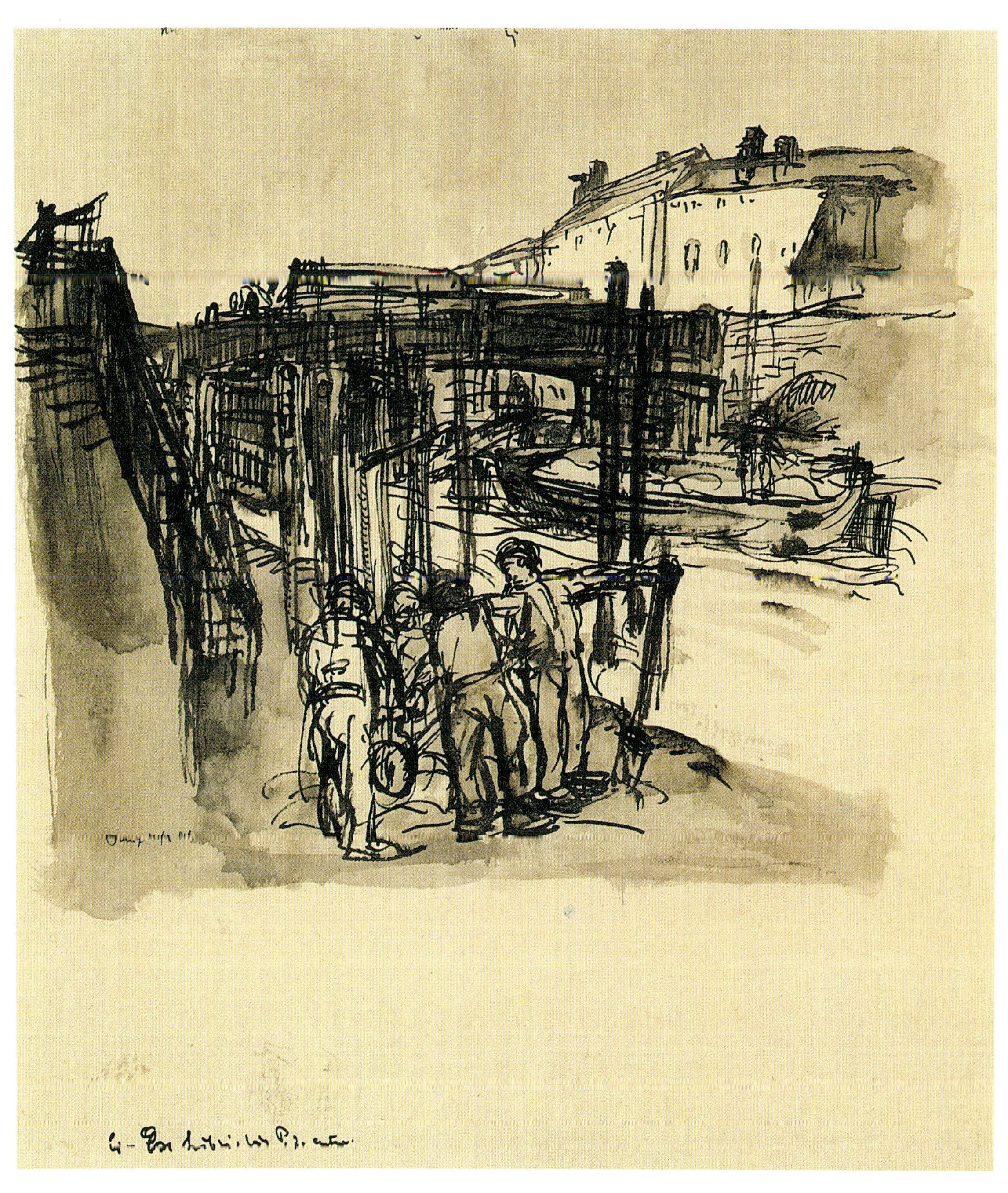

Egon Hofmann

Born Linz, 1884
died Linz, 1972
Descendant of a manufacturer in Linz. Youth and education in Linz. From 1903 studied law at the Universities of Munich, Vienna and Innsbruck. 1908 graduation Dr. jur. et rer. pol., University of Innsbruck. 1909—12 attended Kunsthochschule (Art Academy) in Stuttgart, contact with Hölzel and his circle.
1912 first exhibition in Chemnitz.
1912—15 attended Academy in Dresden and the Academie de la grande Chaumière in Paris. 1915—18 volunteer in World War One, mountain unit. 1919 co-founder with Klemens Brosch of the art association "Der Ring". 1921 co-founder of the art association "MAERZ", its president for many years.
1934 sudden death of his brother forced him to manage the family cement factory at Kirchdorf an der Krems.
1953 member of the Wiener Secession until his death in 1972. Beside his activities as painter, draftsman and graphic artist Egon Hofmann was poet and scholar.

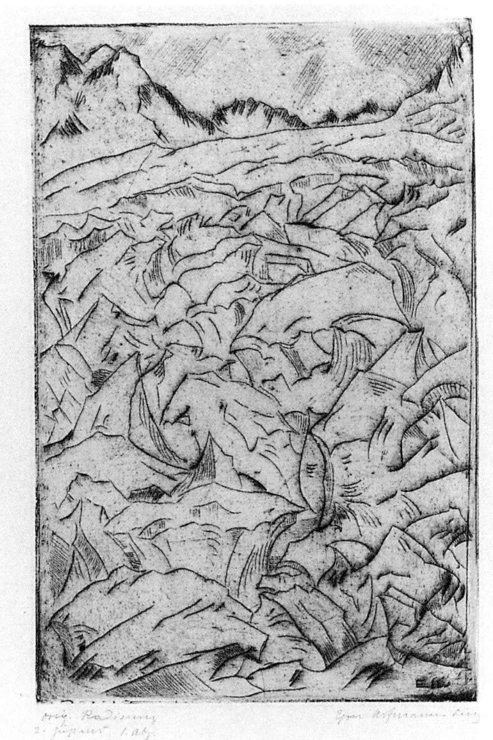

20

Egon Hofmann
Barn in the Snow, ca. 1950—20
color woodcut, 21,7 x 29 cm
Inv.Nr. 4241

21

Egon Hofmann
Untitled, ca. 1915—20
color woodcut, 16,5 x 24 cm
Inv.Nr. 4242

22

Egon Hofmann
Glacier Split, ca. 1920
etching, 24,6 x 16,1 to 40 x 28 cm
Inv.Nr. 4248

Cat. 22

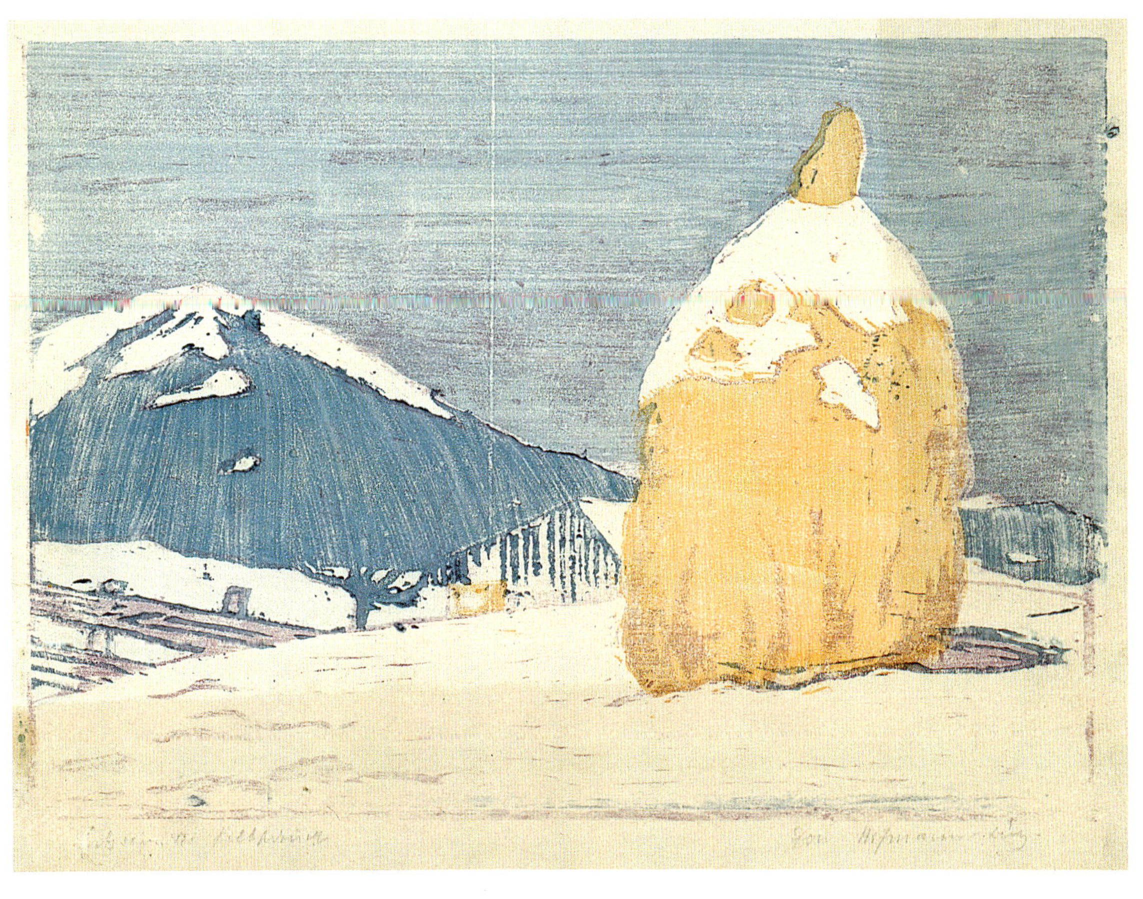

Cat. 20

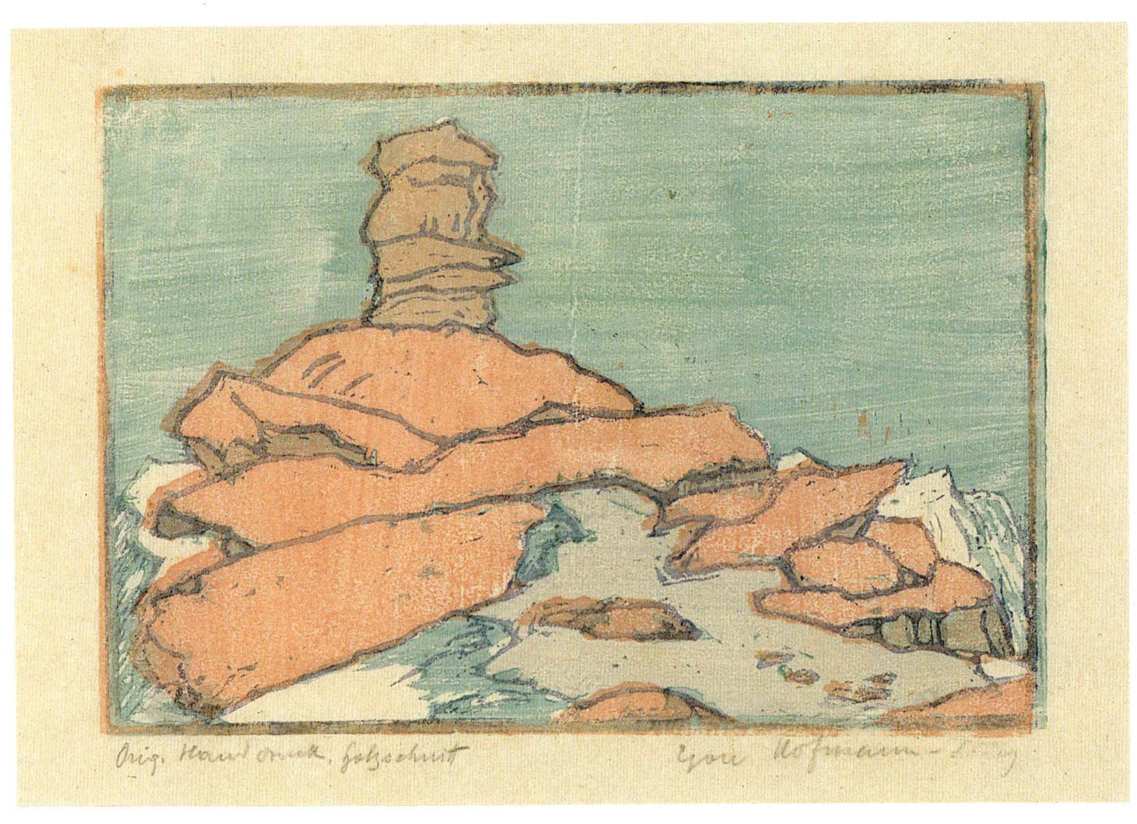

Cat. 21

50

Ludwig Heinrich Jungnickel

Born Wunsiedel, Upper Franconia, 1881
died Vienna, 1965
1885 moved to Munich. Extensive travel in his youth,
to Rome and Naples, etc. Lived from the sale of his
own copies of famous paintings as well as his
portraits. 1899 moved to Vienna where he enrolled at
the Academy. As at previous art schools he could not
bear formal studies. Can be considered autodidactic.
Acquainted with artists associated with Gustav Klimt,
Josef Hoffmann, Kolo Moser, Oskar Kokoschka and
Egon Schiele; some of them were his personal
friends. He lived in the following places which testify
to his restlessness: 1905 back in Munich, 1906 in
Vienna, 1908 second study trip to Rome. 1908
exhibited in the "Kunstschau" in Vienna and made
blueprints for the animal frieze for the Palais Stoclet in
Brussels, a prestigious project of the Wiener
Werkstätte. Further work with the Wiener Werkstätte.
Exhibited woodcuts, brush- and ink-drawings which
made his reputation.
After military service in World War One, he traveled in
Europe, predominantly in Italy and Yugoslavia. When
branded by the Nazis as a "degenerate artist", he
emigrated to Yugoslavia. 1952 returned from Abbazia
to Austria and lived for the rest of his life in Villach and
Vienna.
Jungnickel established his favorite topics early on:
landscapes and animal studies. In his early period, he
was influenced by Art Nouveau; in the interwar
period, he developed his particular style: the essence
of motifs is rendered with undulating and curved lines
and splotches of color.

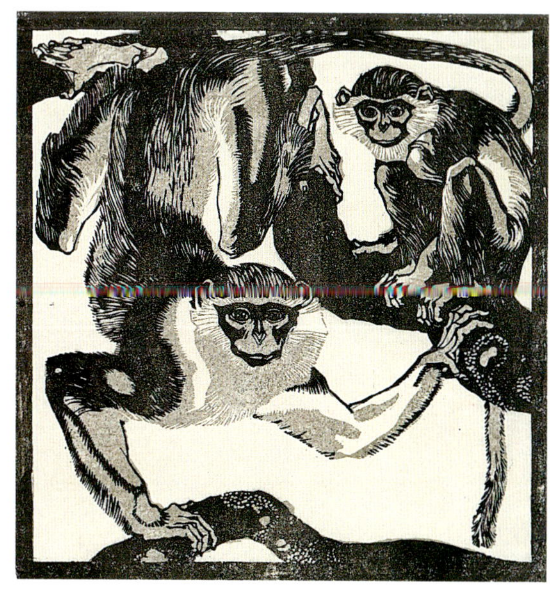

Cat. 24

23

Ludwig Heinrich Jungnickel
Pair of Tigers, 1905/06
stencil, 32,9 x 36 to 38,1 x 36,5 cm
Inv.Nr. 1237

24

Ludwig Heinrich Jungnickel
Mother Ape with Young, ca. 1910
woodcut, 30 x 28,2 to 32,7 x 29,3
Inv.Nr. 1236

25

Ludwig Heinrich Jungnickel
Polo Player, ca. 1920
charcoal on paper, 35,7 x 45,3 cm
Inv.Nr. 2823

26

Ludwig Heinrich Jungnickel
Lion Hunt, ca. 1920
washed and aquarelled charcoal,
39 x 54,5 cm
Inv.Nr. 3503

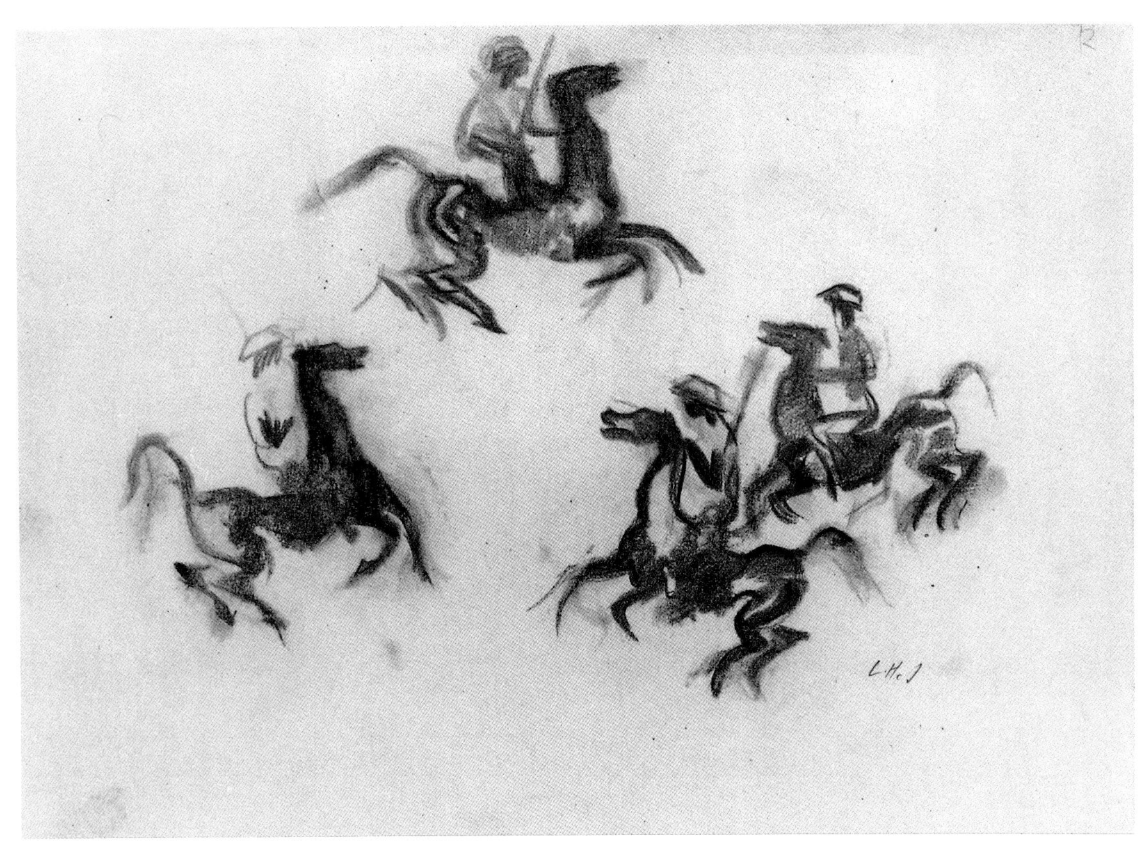

Cat. 25

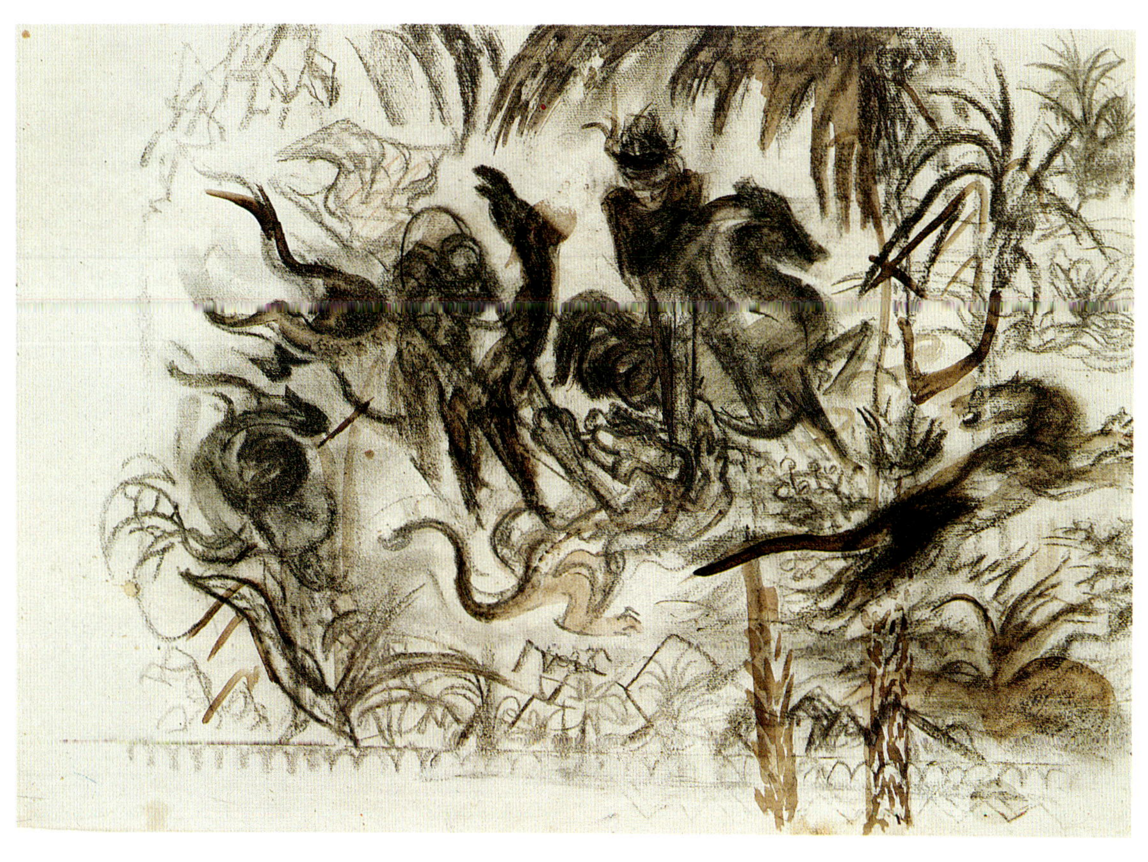

Cat. 26

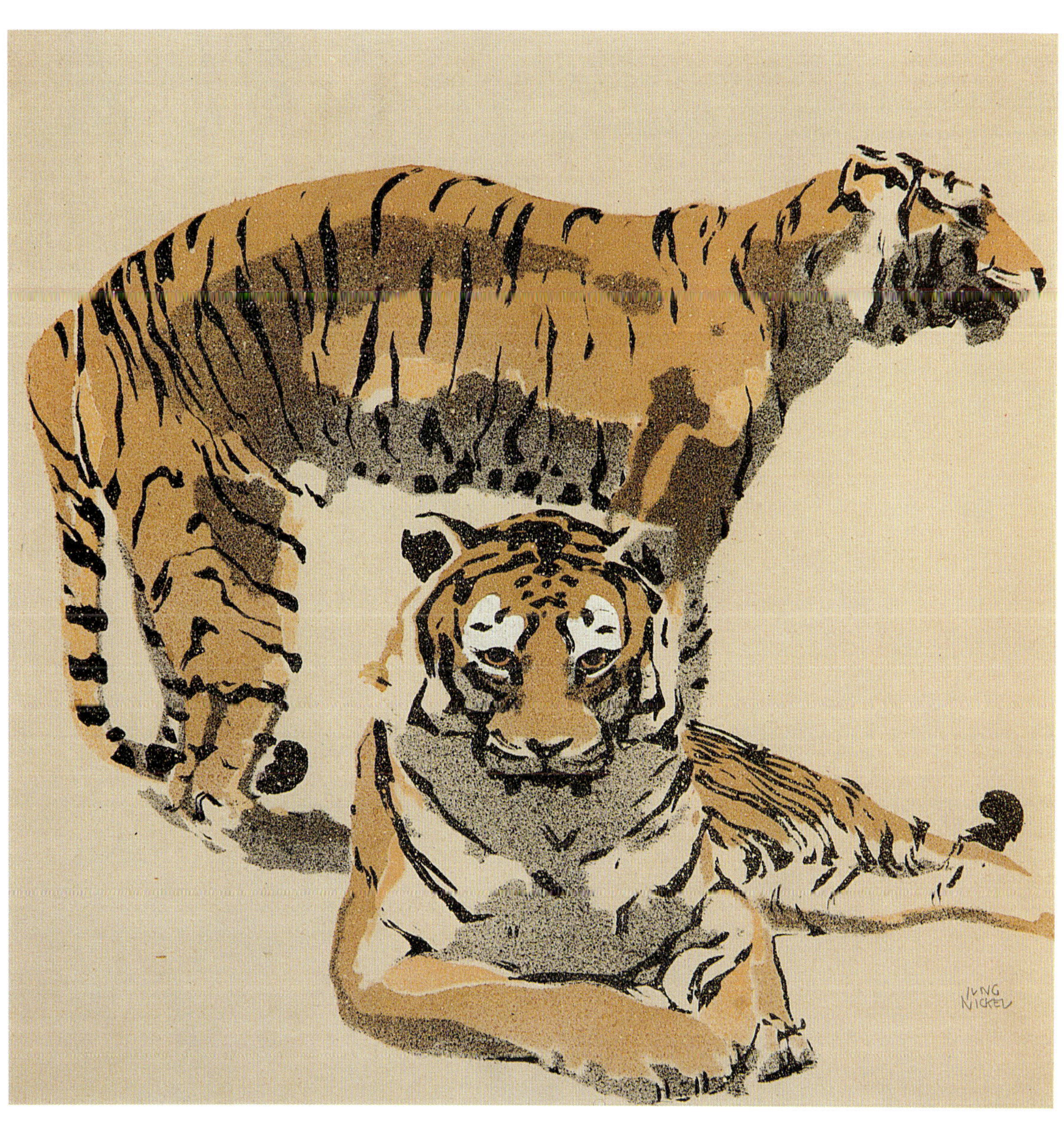

Cat. 23

Gustav Klimt

Painter and graphic artist, born on July 14, 1862 in Vienna, died February 6, 1918 in Vienna.

1876 — 1883 he was a student with Karl Hrachowina, Ludwig Minnigerode, Michael Rieser, but mainly with Ferdinand Julius Laufberger at the "Wiener Kunst-gewerbeschule" and with Julius Victor Berger at the Vienna Academy. He shared a studio with Ernst Klimt and Franz Matsch, while working on major decorative commissions until the death of Ernst Klimt in 1892.

Municipal Theaters in Fiume (Rijeka) and Karlsbad (Karlovy Vary), and the Burgtheater and Kunsthistorische Museum (Museum of Fine Arts) in Vienna.

In 1897, he was the most important founding member of the Secession, als well as its first president, a position he held until 1899. From 1900 to 1903, Klimt completed and eventually exhibited the famous "Fakultätsbilder" (Faculty Paintings) intended for the "Aula" (large auditorium) of the Vienna University, leading to a major public scandal because of the — for that time — extreme frankness of representation. In 1900, Klimt was awarded the Gold Medal for his Faculty Painting "Philosophy" at the Paris World Exhibition.

In 1905, Klimt, was well as a group of likewise-minded members, seceded from the Secession ("Klimt-Group").

1908 he was chosen to made the opening speech at the "Kunstschau", travelled to Paris in 1909, and participated in the Venice "Biennale" in 1910. In 1911 and 1914, his works were shown at the International Art Exhibits in Rome. In 1911 Klimt also had shows in Brussels, London and Madrid.

In 1912, he became president of the Austrian "Künstlerbund", and since 1917 had been an honorary member of the Academies of Fine Arts both in Vienna and in Munich.

27

Gustav Klimt
Singer (Study for Portrait of Frau von Rosthorn), about 1901
lead pencil and blue pencil on paper, 44,6 x 31 cm
Inv.Nr. 558

28

Gustav Klimt
Seated Woman, 1910
pencil on pseudo-japan paper, 37 x 56 cm
Inv.Nr. 1227

29

Gustav Klimt
Study for a Portrait of a Woman, about 1914
pencil on wrapping paper, 57 x 37,5 cm
Inv.Nr. 560

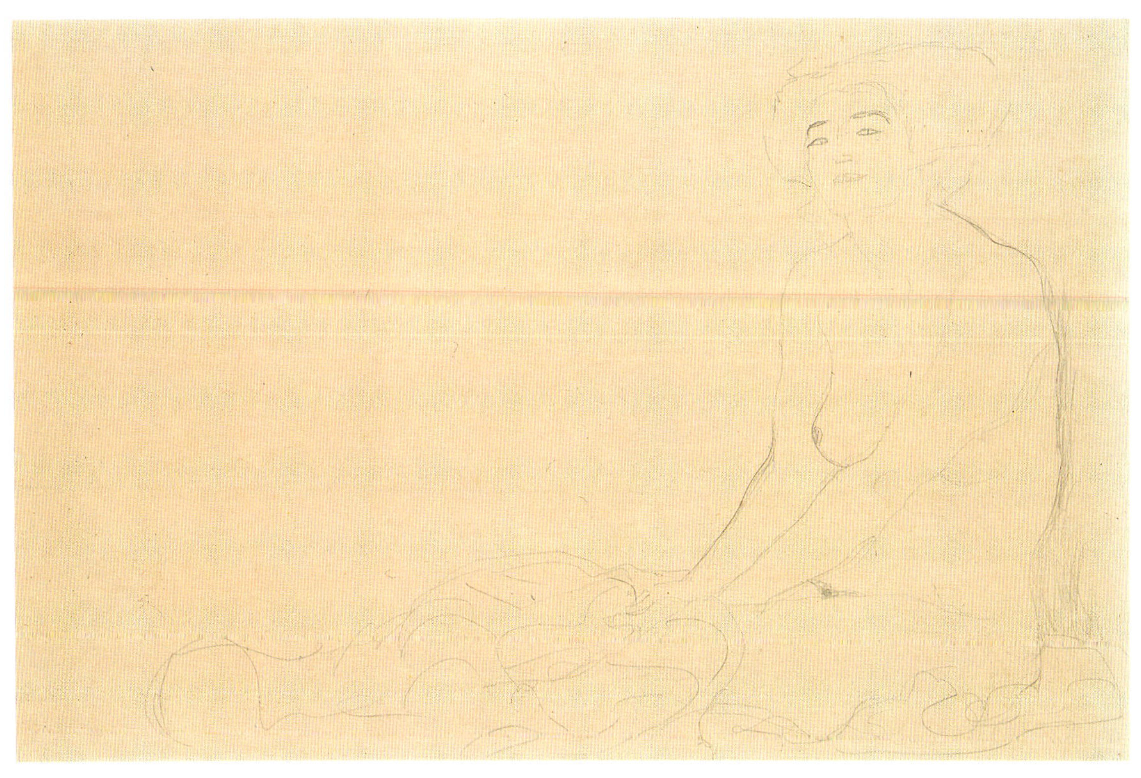

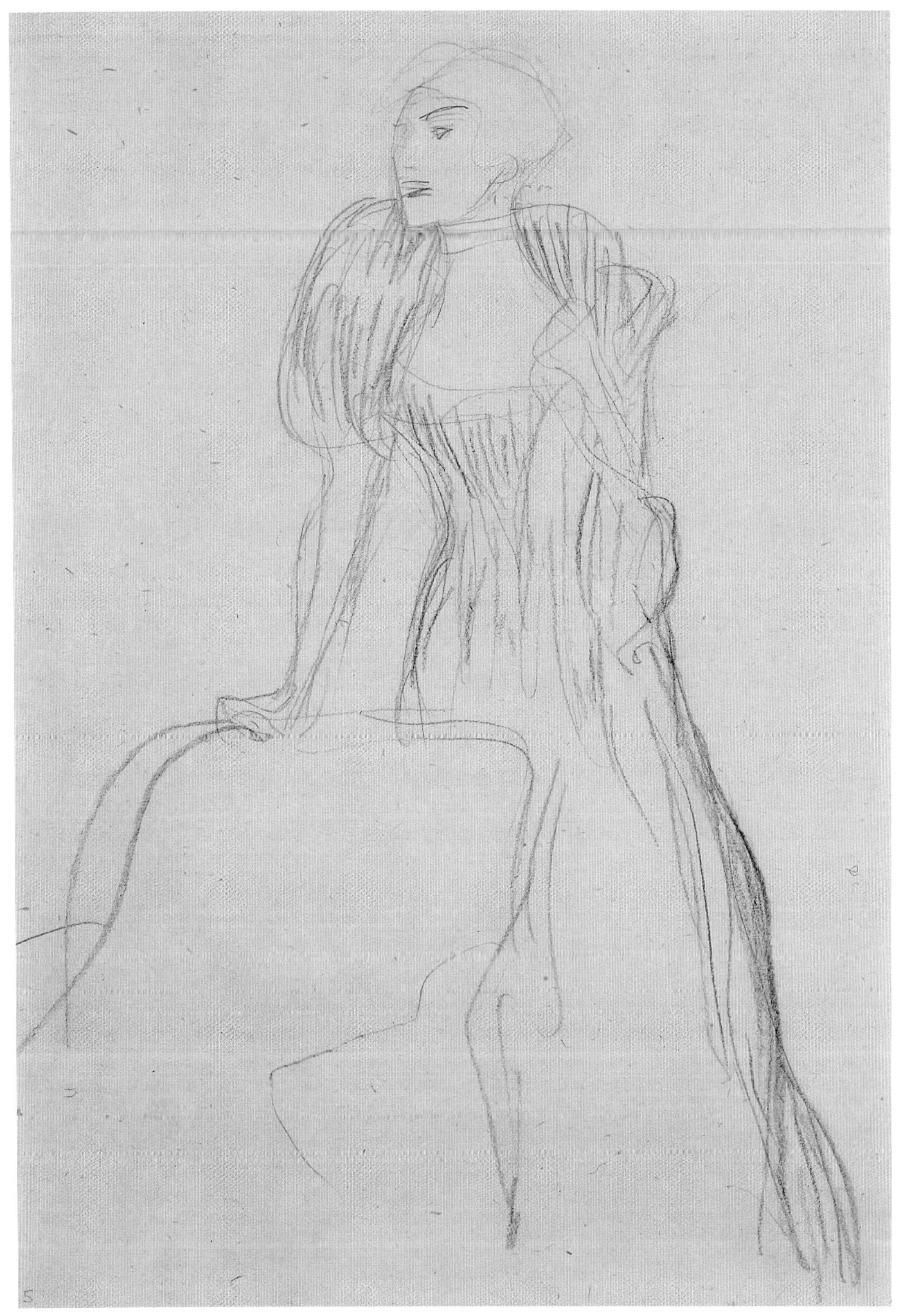

Cat. 29

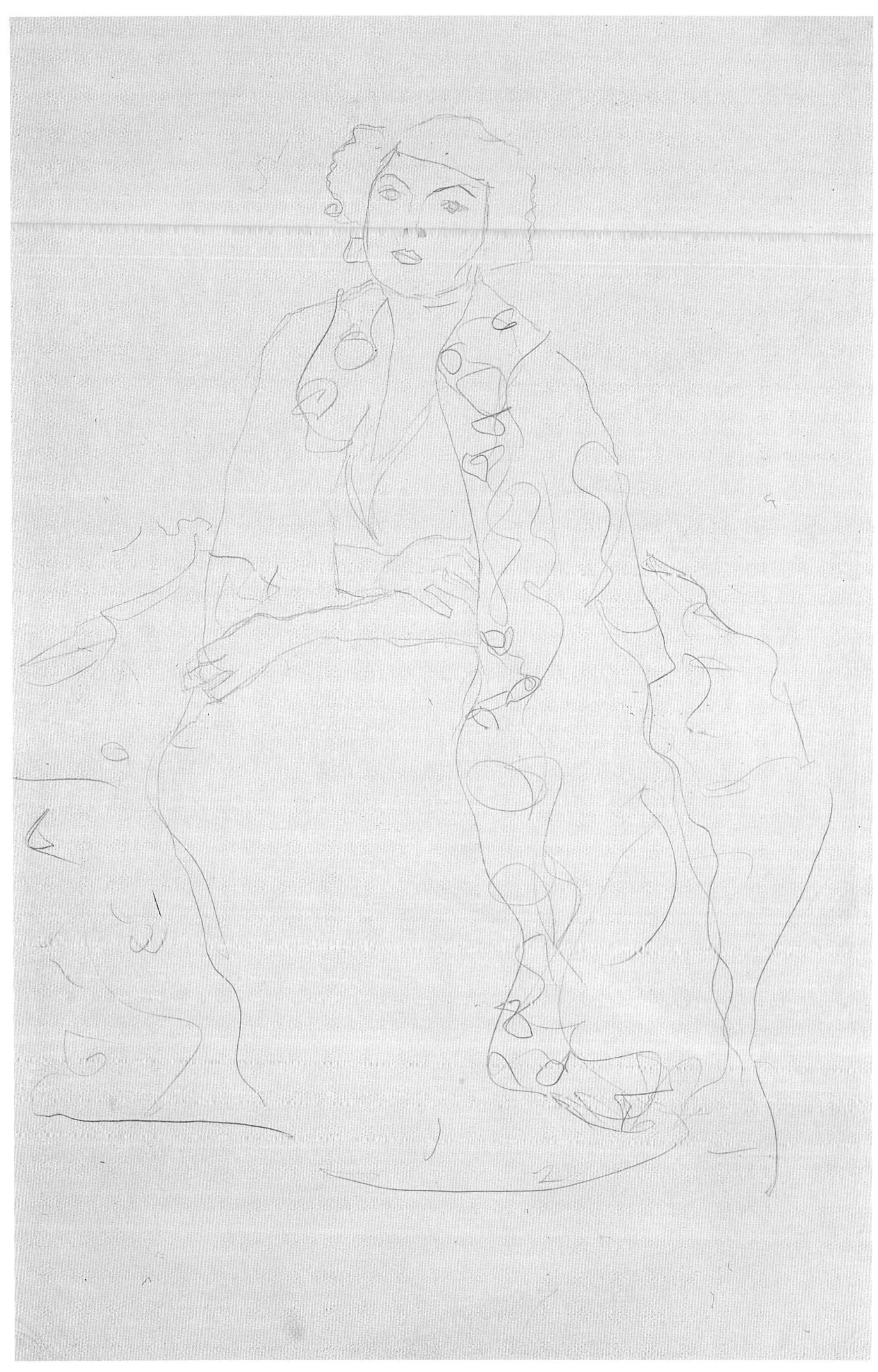

Oskar Kokoschka

Born on March 1, 1886 in Pöchlarn, Austria, died on
February 22, 1980, in Montreux, France.

1905—   Studies at the "Wiener Kunstgewerbe-
1909   schule", (Vienna School of Arts and Crafts)
        tutored by Mallina, Czeschka, von Kenner,
        Löffler.

1907—   Member of the "Wiener Werkstätte".
1909   Kokoschka's friendship with Adolf Loos and
        Karl Kraus started in 1908.
        In the same year, als well as in 1909, Oscar
        Kokoschka participated in the
        "Kunstschau". Stayed in Berlin, contributed
        to the avantgarde periodical "Der Sturm";
        signed a contract with Cassierer.

1911/12 Assistent of Prof. Kenner at the "Wiener
        Kunstgewerbeschule". Kokoschka meets
        Alma Mahler.

1913   Kokoschka started to teach at the
        "Schwarzwaldschule", a progressive
        educational institution in Vienna. Travels to
        Italy.

After sustaining injuries in World War I (1915),
Kokoschka worked and taught in Vienna and Dresden
(since 1917).

1919—   Professor at the Academy of Fine Arts in
1924   Dresden. Kokoschka submitted work to the
        Biennale in Venice. He participated again
        both in 1932 and 1948.

1924—   He made his home in Paris, a stay that was
1933   interrupted by many journeys, e.g. to
        London, Spain, Berlin, Tunis, Egypt,
        Ireland, Scotland, and Italy.

1933/34 Stay in Vienna; subsequently in Prague.

1938—   Flight to London. Stays in Scotland. —
1947   Since 1947 British subject.

1953   Founded the "School of Seeing" in
        Salzburg.
        He moved to Villeneuve on Lake Geneva.

1957   Stays in Salzburg, England and Italy.

1961—   Travels in Greece, Apulia and Morocco.
1965

DIE TRÄUMENDEN
KNABEN.

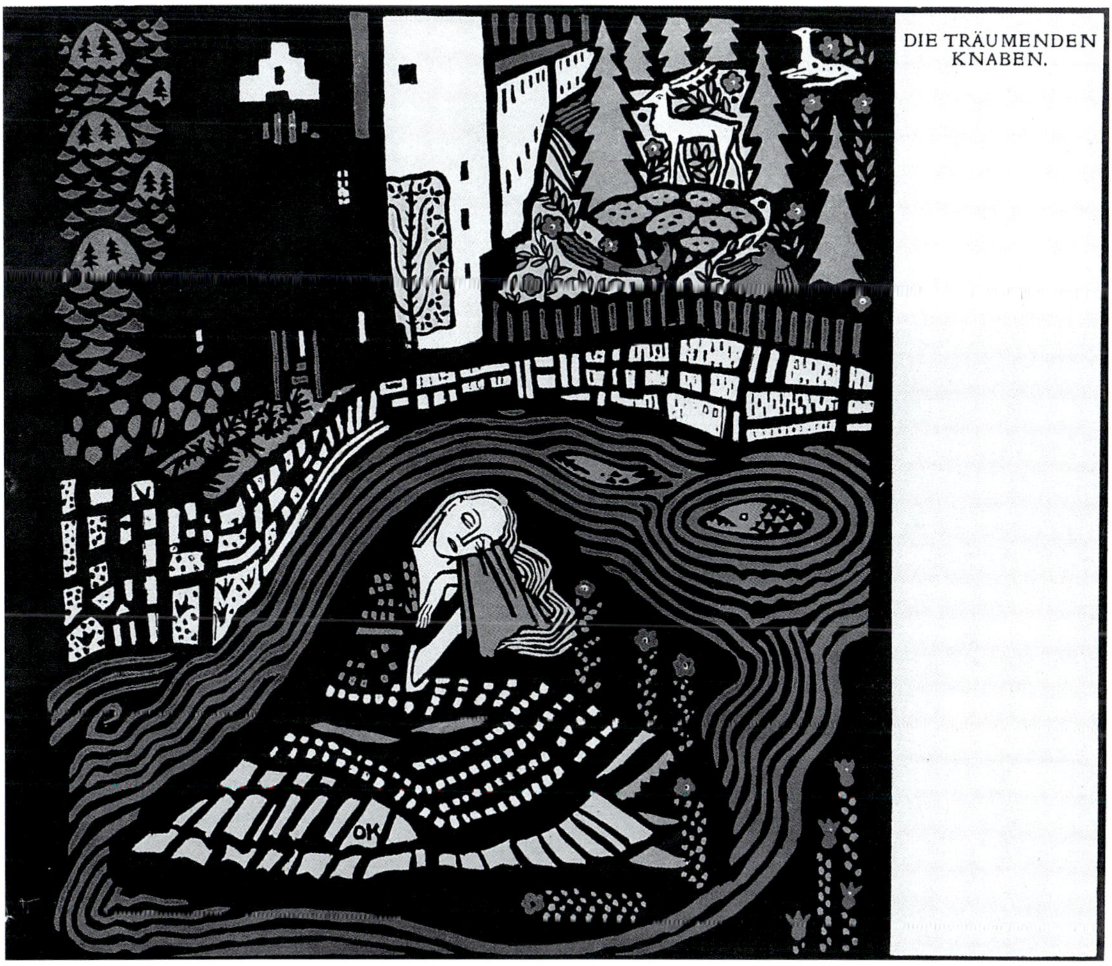

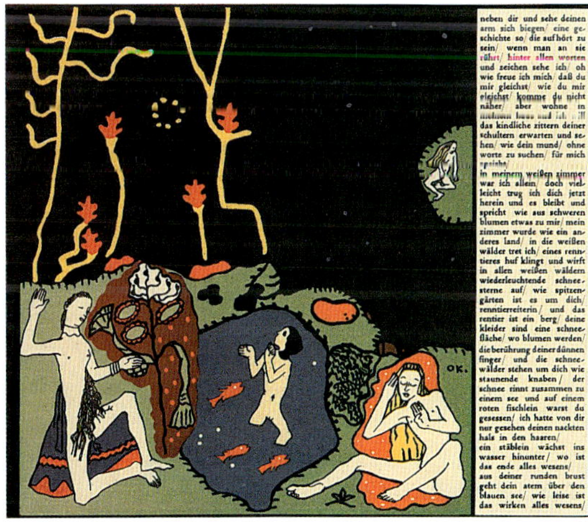

neben dir und sehe deinen
arm sich biegen/ eine ge-
schichte so/ die aufhört zu
sein/ wenn man an sie
rührt/ hinter allen worten
und zeichen sehe ich/ oh
wie freue ich mich/ daß du
mir gleichst/ wie du mir
gleichst/ komme du nicht
näher/ aber wohne in
meinem haus und ich will
das kindliche zittern deiner
schultern erwarten und se-
hen/ wie dein mund/ ohne
worte zu suchen/ für mich
spricht/
in meinem weißen zimmer
war ich allein/ doch viel-
leicht trug ich dich jetzt
herein und es bleibt und
spricht wie aus schweren
blumen etwas zu mir/ mein
zimmer wurde wie ein an-
deres land/ in die weißen
wälder tret ich/ eines renn-
tieres huf klingt und wirft
in allen weißen wäldern
wiederleuchtende schnee-
sterne auf/ wie spitzen-
gärten ist es um dich/
renntierreiterin/ und das
rentier ist ein berg/ deine
kleider sind eine schnee-
fläche/ wo blumen werden/
die berührung deiner dünnen
finger/ und die schnee-
wälder stehen um dich wie
staunende knaben/ der
schnee rinnt zusammen zu
einem see und auf einem
roten fischlein warst du
gesessen/ ich hatte von dir
nur gesehen deinen nackten
hals in den haaren/
ein stäblein wächst ins
wasser hinunter/ wo ist
das ende alles wesens/
aus deiner runden brust
geht dein atem über den
blauen see/ wie leise ist
das wirken alles wesens/

Cat. 32   Cat. 30

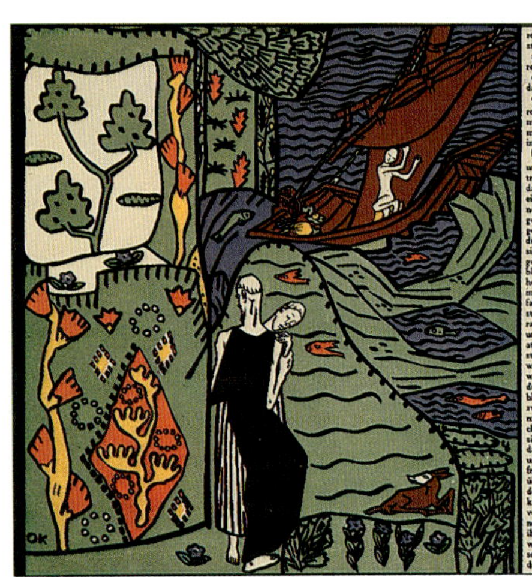

rot fischlein/ fischlein rot,
stech dich mit dem drei-
schneidigen messer tot
reiß dich mit meinen fingern
entzwei/
daß dem stummen kreisen
ein ende sei/
rot fischlein/ fischlein rot/
mein messerlein ist rot/
meine fingerlein sind rot/
in der schale sinkt ein
fischlein tot/

und ich fiel nieder und
träumte/ viele taschen hat
das schicksal/ ich warte bei
einem peruanischen steiner-
nen baum/ seine vielfingri-
gen blätterarme greifen wie
geängstigte arme und finger
dünner/ gelber figuren/ die
sich in dem sternblumigen
gebüsch unmerklich wie
blinde rühren/ ohne daß ein
heller/ verziehender streifen
in der dunklen luft von
fallenden sternblumen die
stummen tiere lockt/ blut-
raserinnen/ die zu vieren
und fünfen aus den grünen/
atmenden seewäldern/wo es
still regnet/ wegschleichen/
wellen schlagen über die
wälder hinweg und gehen
durch die wurzellosen/ rot-
blumigen/ unzähligen luft-
zweige/ die wie haare im
meerwasser saugend tau-
chen/ dort heraus winden
sich die grünen wogen/ und
das schreckliche meer der
untiefen und menschen-
fressenden fische/ faßt die
überfüllte galeere /oben an
den masten schwingen
käfige mit kleinen blauen
vögeln/ zieht an den eiser-
nen ketten und tanzt mit
ihr hinein in die teifune, wo
wassersäulen wie geister-
schlangen auf dem brüllen-
den meer gehen/ ich höre

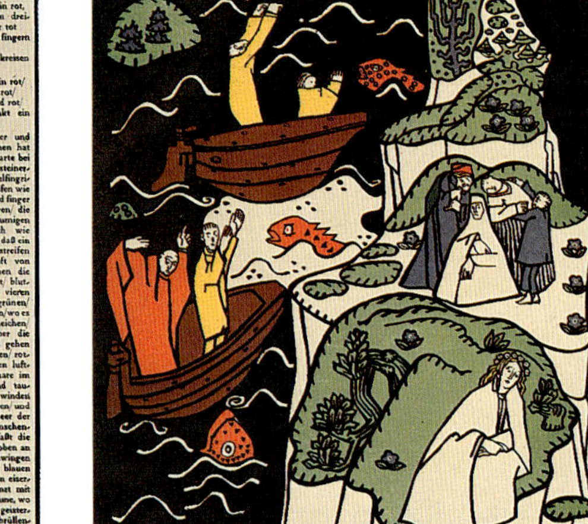

die rufe der schiffer/ die
in die länder der sprechen-
den vögel wollen/ die
segel schwankten hin und
schwankten her/ kalte luft
bewegte sie und drehte die
tücher/ das schiff legt an/
leise gehen taktmäßig/ in
pausen verständlich/ dann
wieder übertönt die pro-
zessionen der vom schiff
steigenden/ schleicher in
braunen wollkleidern win-
den sich durch und nackte
magere mädchen geben
vögel/ nüsse und korallen-
schnüre zur erinnerung an
die nächte der dunklen zärt-
lichkeiten/ und ich fiel
und träumte die kranke
nacht/

was schlaft ihr/ blauge-
kleidete männer/ unter den
zweigen der dunklen nuß-
bäume im mondlicht?

ihr milden frauen/ was quillt
in euren roten mänteln/ in
den leibern die erwartung
verschlungener glieder seit
gestern und jeher?

spürt ihr die aufgeregte
wärme der zittrigen/ lauen
luft — ich bin der kreisen-
de wärwolf —

wenn die abendglocke ver-
tönt/ schleich ich in eure
gärten/ in eure weiden/
breche ich in euren fried-
lichen kraal/

mein abgezäumter körper/
mein mit blut und farbe
erhöhter körper/ kriecht in
eure laubhütten/ schwärmt
durch eure dörfer/ kriecht
in eure seelen/ schwärt in
euren leibern/

aus der einsamsten stille/
vor eurem erwachen gellt
mein geheul/

Cat. 31

Cat. 34

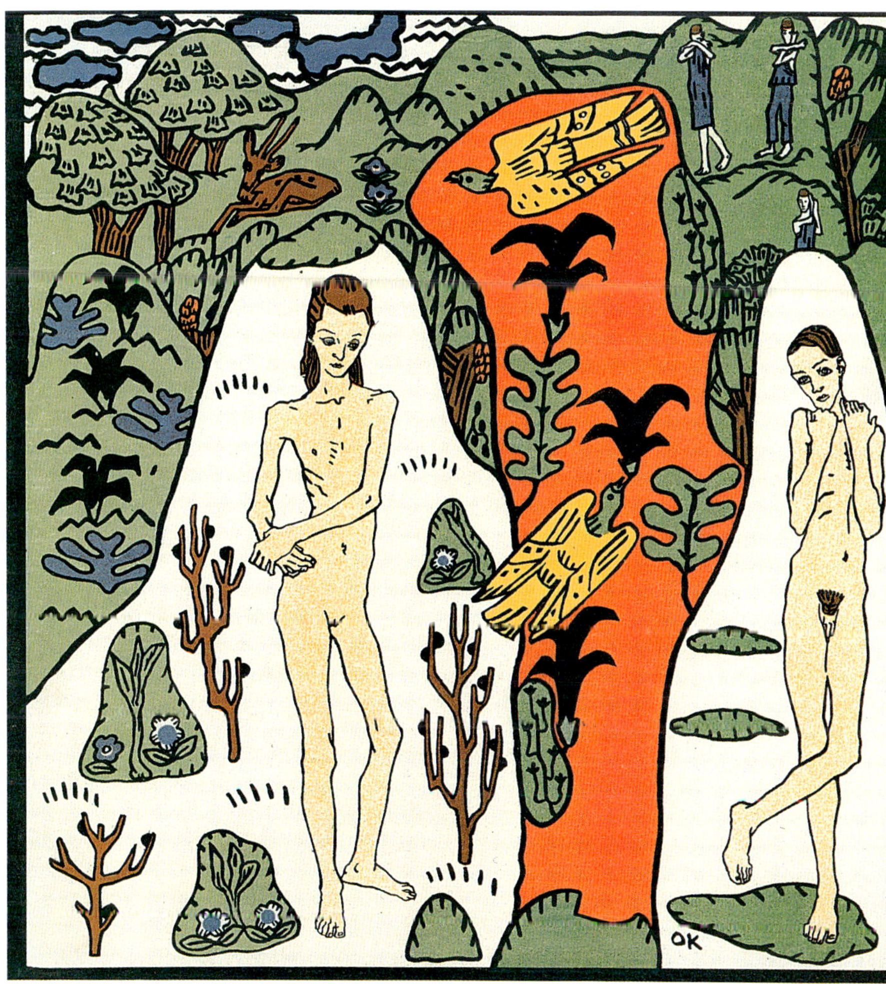

ich greife in den see und
tauche in deinen haaren/
wie ein versonnener bin
ich in der liebe alles wesens/
und wieder fiel ich nieder
und träumte/
zu viel hitze überkam mich
in der nacht/ da in den wäldern die paarende schlange
ihre haut streicht unter dem
heißen stein und der wasser-
hirsch reibt sein gehörn
an den zimmtstauden/ als
ich den moschus des tieres
ruh in allen niedrigen
sträuchern/
es ist fremd um mich/ je-
mand sollte antworten/
alles läuft nach seinen ei-
genen fährten/ und die
singenden mücken über-
zittern die schreie/
wer denkt grinsende götter-
gesichter und fragt den sing-
sang der zauberer und alt-
männer/ wenn sie die boot-
fahrer begleiten/ welche
frauen holen/
und ich war ein kriechend
ding/ als ich die tiere suchte
und mich zu ihnen hielt/
kleiner/ was wolltest du
hinter den alten/ als du die
gottzauberer aufsuchtest/
und ich war ein taumelnder/
als ich mein fleisch er-
kannte/
und ein allesliebender/ als
ich mit einem mädchen
sprach/

dieses buch wurde geschrie-
ben und gezeichnet von
Oskar Kokoschka/ verlegt
von der wiener werkstätte/
gedruckt in den offizinen
Berger und Chwala/ 1908

Cat. 33

65

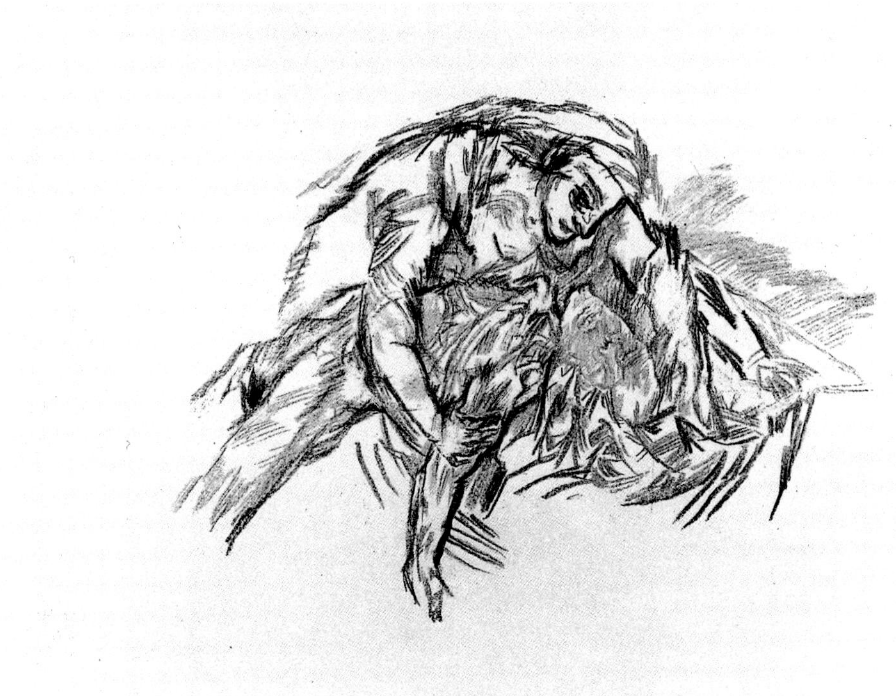

Cat. 36

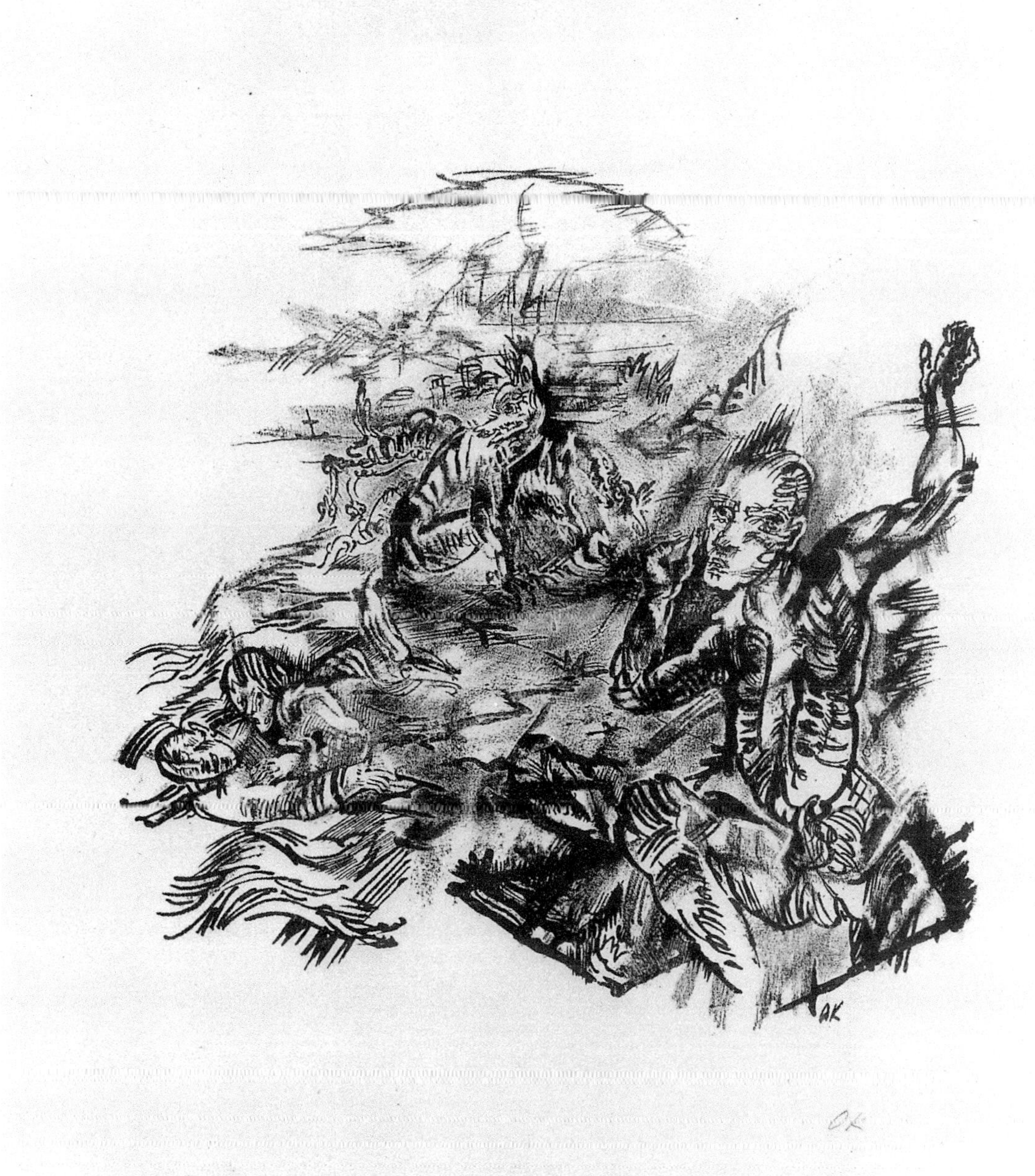

Cat. 35

67

30

Oskar Kokoschka
The Dreaming Boys I (Sleeping), 1908
color lithograph in five colors, 24 x 29 cm
Inv.Nr. 490

31

Oskar Kokoschka
The Dreaming Boys II, 1908
color lithograph in five colors, 24 x 29 cm
Inv.Nr. 491

32

Oskar Kokoschka
The Dreaming Boys VII, 1906—08
color lithograph in five colors, 24 x 29 cm
Inv.Nr. 496

33

Oskar Kokoschka
*The Dreaming Boys VIII
(The Girl Li and Myself), 1906—08*
color lithograph in six colors, 24 x 29 cm
Inv.Nr. 497

34

Oskar Kokoschka
*The Dreaming Boys III
(The Boatsmen Calling), 1908*
color lithograph in five colors, 24 x 29 cm
Inv.Nr. 492

35

Oskar Kokoschka
*Walk into Grave
(from: The Chained Columbus), 1913/16*
lithograph, 49,5 x 39 cm
Inv.Nr. 5075

36

Oskar Kokoschka
*Woman Bent over Schemes
(from: The Chained Columbus)*
lithograph, 35 x 48 cm
Inv.Nr. 5076

37

Oskar Kokoschka
Max Reinhardt, 1919
color lithograph, 38,6 x 30,3 cm
Inv.Nr. 490

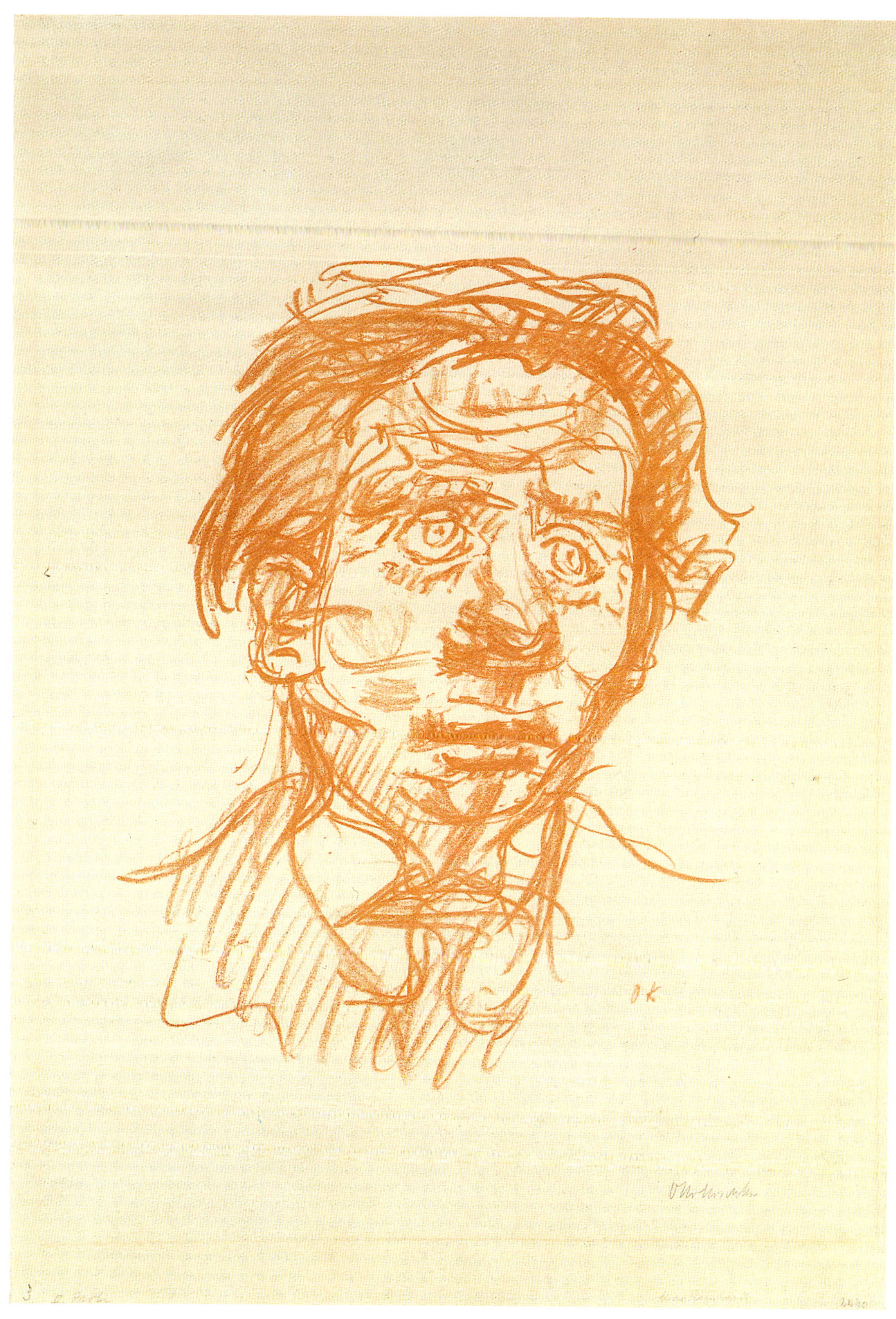

Cat. 37

Broncia Koller-Pinell

Born Sanok, Galicia, 23. 2. 1863
died Oberwaltersdorf, Lower Austria, 26. 3. 1934
Her father, Saul Pineles, was an architect of military
fortifications. 1870 moved to Vienna with family.
Studied with sculptor J. Raab, then with the painter A.
Delug; chose the artist's name Pinell. 1885—90 lived
in Munich, studied at the Academy with L. Herterich.
1894 participated in a group exhibition in the
Künstlerhaus, Vienna. Her early painting "Adagio"
was later acquired by S. Freud. Met the physicist and
physician Dr. Hugo Koller, a friend of the composer
Hugo Wolf; they married in 1896 and moved to
Golling (Salzburg), then to Nuremberg. Their
daughter Sylvia, born in 1898, became also a painter.
In Nuremberg Broncia Koller-Pinell studied engraving
techniques.
1903 returned to Vienna, after 1904 lived most of their
time on their estate in Oberwaltersdorf, south of
Vienna, inherited from her father. Kolo Moser and
Josef Hoffmann redesigned the house and furnished
the rooms. Their estate was a social gathering place
for philosophers, musicians, scholars, and artists of
the Wiener Werkstätte, for Klimt and his friends.
Represented at the first "Kunstschau" in 1908;
member of the Münchner Künstlergenossenschaft
where she exhibited several times. Regular
exhibitions after World War One.
Her husband was one of the major Viennese art
sponsors at the time. Artists of the younger generation
such as A. P. Gütersloh, E. Schiele, G. Mahler, and P.
Hindemith were regular guests in Oberwaltersdorf.
1918 Schiele portrayed Dr. Koller, while she painted
the Schieles. From 1924 close contacts to the Berlin
art scene via Carl Hofer.
Despite her close ties to Klimt, his influence is
manifest only in a few of her paintings. More than most
other Viennese artists, she reacted to international
trends. This accounts for a visible disparity in her
oeuvre: the influence of Bonnard and Vuillard (their
emphasis on color, for example) and the impact of
Kolo Moser or Ferdinand Andri in her woodcuts which
belong to the best of this period.

38

Broncia Koller-Pinell
Sleeping Girl (Silvia Koller), 1903/04
woodcut in two colors on japanese paper,
26 x 31 cm (portfolio with 10 woodcuts)
Inv.Nr. 3098

39

Broncia Koller-Pinell
The Mother of the Artist, 1903/04
woodcut on japanese paper, 36 x 31 cm
Inv.Nr. 3091

40

Broncia Koller-Pinell
Eve, 1903/04
woodcut in two colors, 34,6 x 24 cm
(portfolio with 10 woodcuts)
Inv.Nr. 3095

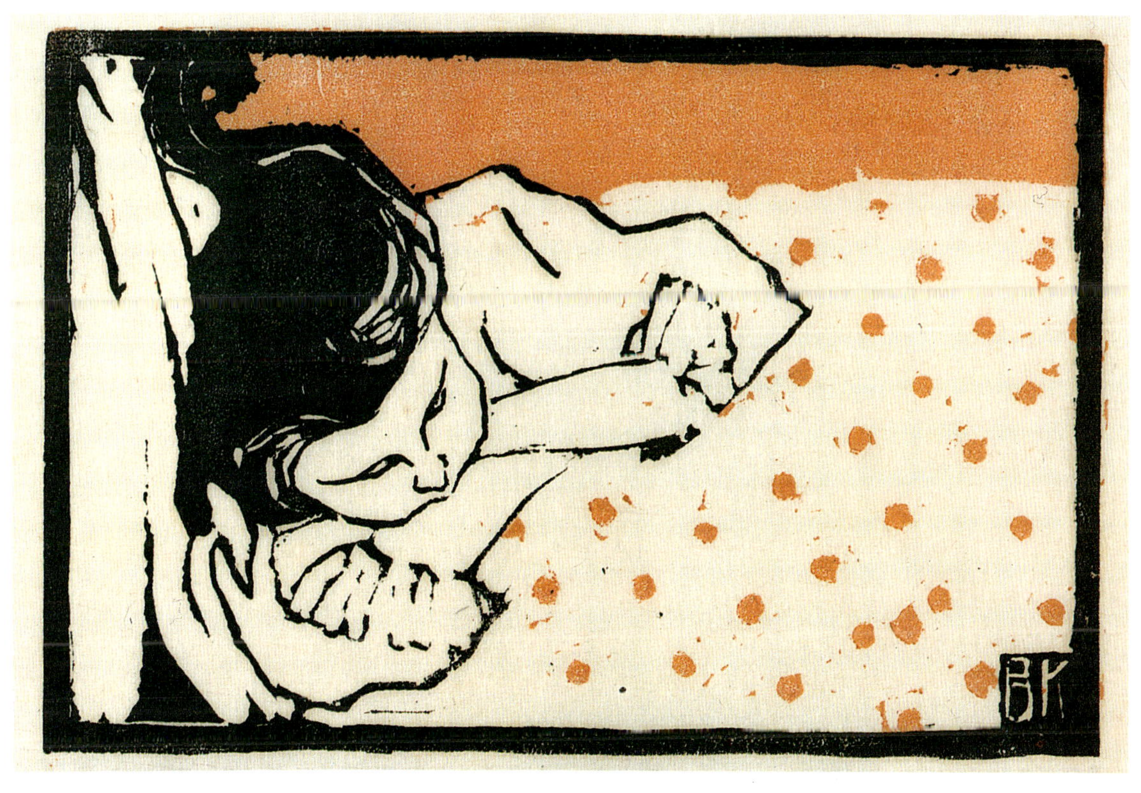

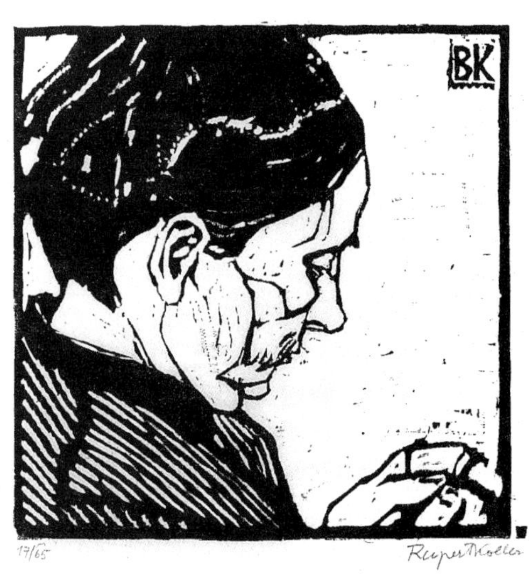

Cat. 39

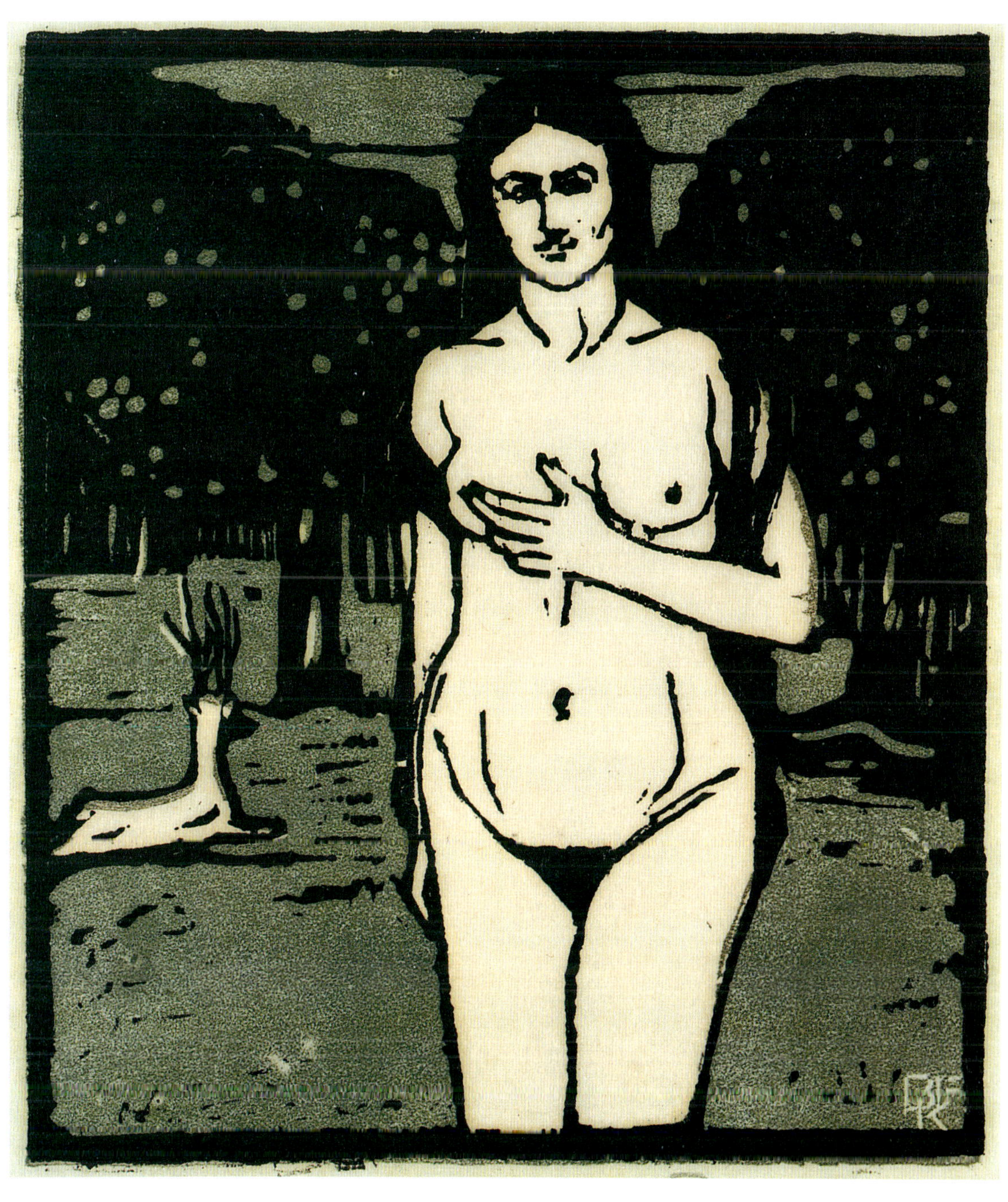

Cat. 40

73

Anton Kolig

Born Neutitschein, Northern Moravia, 1886
died Nötsch im Gailtal, Carinthia. 1950
Son of a house-painter from Northern Moravia; grew up in Vienna. 1904—06 studied at the Wiener Kunstgewerbeschule (applied arts), 1907—12 Vienna Academy. 1911 participated with O. Kokoschka, A. Faistauer, A. P. Gütersloh, F. Wiegele and Isepp in the Sonderbundausstellung of the Hagenbund.
1912—14 studied in Paris. War painter during World War One, residence in Nötsch, Carinthia. 1928 appointed Professor at the Württembergische Kunstakademie in Stuttgart where he taught until 1943. Return to Nötsch. Seriously wounded during an Allied air attack, during which his brother-in-law, the painter Franz Wiegele was killed. Despite lasting disability continuation of his artistic career.
His name is intimately connected with the "Nötscher Kreis", a loose association of the artists Kolig, Isepp, Wiegele, Esterl, Boeckl, Frankl, who never thought of themselves as a formal group but due to their vivid and artistic discourse were cited as "Nötscher Kreis".
Kolig's work up to World War One show his preoccupation with Austrian and French modern painting. In this period, still lifes prevail with color determining substantially the structure of a composition. During the war, especially in the early twenties, he was occupied with the human figure. His expressive command of male nudes reflects his fascination with Michelangelo.
The plasticity of his late period is best documented in preparatory sketches he did for the frescos for the Vienna Crematorium of for the 1927 mosaic of the Festival Hall in Salzburg, neither of which unfortunately were executed.
Throughout his life Kolig experimented in various fields. With new color cohesives he tried to heighten the luminosity of his pigments.

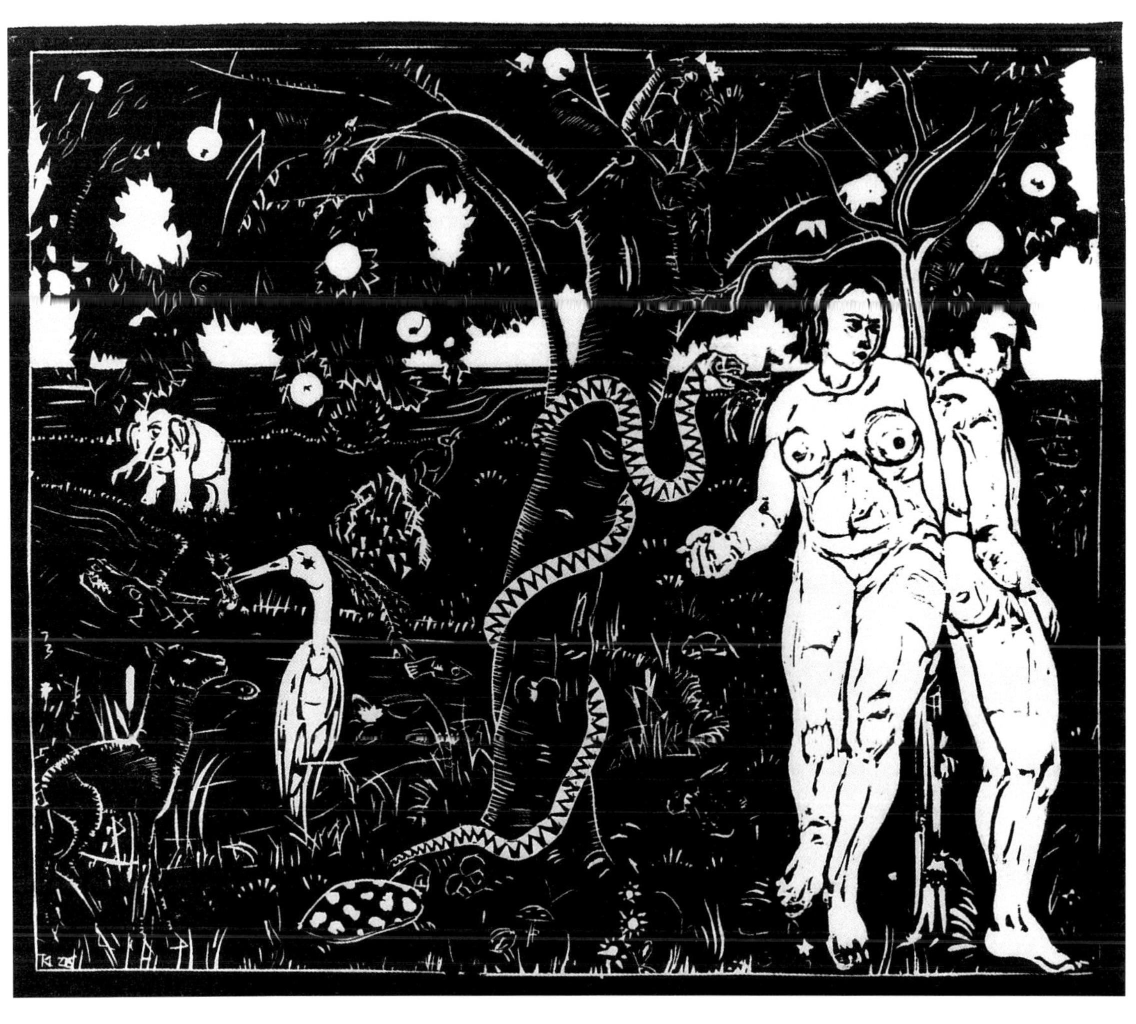

Cat. 41

41

Anton Kolig
Adam and Eve in Paradise, 1905
woodcut, 21 x 24 to 49 x 37 cm
Inv.Nr. 3903

Alfred Kubin

1877	Born on April 10, in Litomerice/Leitmeritz, Bohemia.
1887/88	Attended the "gymnasium" (highschool) in Salzburg.
1891/92	Arts and crafts school in Salzburg.
1892— 1896	Kubin was apprenticed to the photographer Beer in Klagenfurt, Carinthia.
1896	Attempted suicide at his mother's grave in October.
1897	Military service from January to April, terminated by a severe nervous disorder.
1898— 1901	Attended the private art school Schmidt-Reutte and the Gysios Class at the Fine Arts Academy in Munich.
1902	First one-man show with Paul Cassirer in Berlin.
1903	First portfolio: Hans von Weber publishes 15 of Kubin's drawings in the form of heliotype reproductions.
1904	Married Hedwig Gründler in the end of March.
1906	First stay in Paris. In June, Kubin bought the chalet Zwickledt near Wernstein on the Inn, moving there from Munich.
1908	Travels in Upper Italy with Fritz von Herzmanovsky-Orlando. Wrote the important novel "Die andere Seite", which was published by Piper in Munich and Leipzig, with reproductions of 52 of his drawings in 1909.
1912	Joined the Munich "Blauer Reiter" group.
1921	First one-man show at Goltz in Munich.
1930	Becomes a member of the Prussian Academy of Fine Arts in Berlin.
1937	Major one-man show at Vienna's Albertina in honor of his 60th birthday. Kubin was appointed professor that same year.
1947	Kubin was named an Honorary Citizen of the City of Linz.
1948	On August 15, his wife Hedwig died.
1949	Member of the "Bayerische Akademie der Schönen Künste".
1951	Received Austrian State Award for Visual Arts.
1952	Prize at the Biennale in Venice.
1955	Prize at the Biennale in Sao Paulo.
1959	Kubin died in Zwickledt on August 20.

Kubin's significance as an artist lies primarily in his oeuvre of drawings and illustrations. All told, he illustrated more than 200 books and loose-leaf editions. The Oberösterreichische Landesmuseum (Upper Austrian State Museum), the graphic arts collection Albertina in Vienna, and the Neue Galerie in Linz own major portions of originals by Kubin.
Monographs on Alfred Kubin have been published by Hans Bisanz, Wieland Schmid and Alfred Marks.

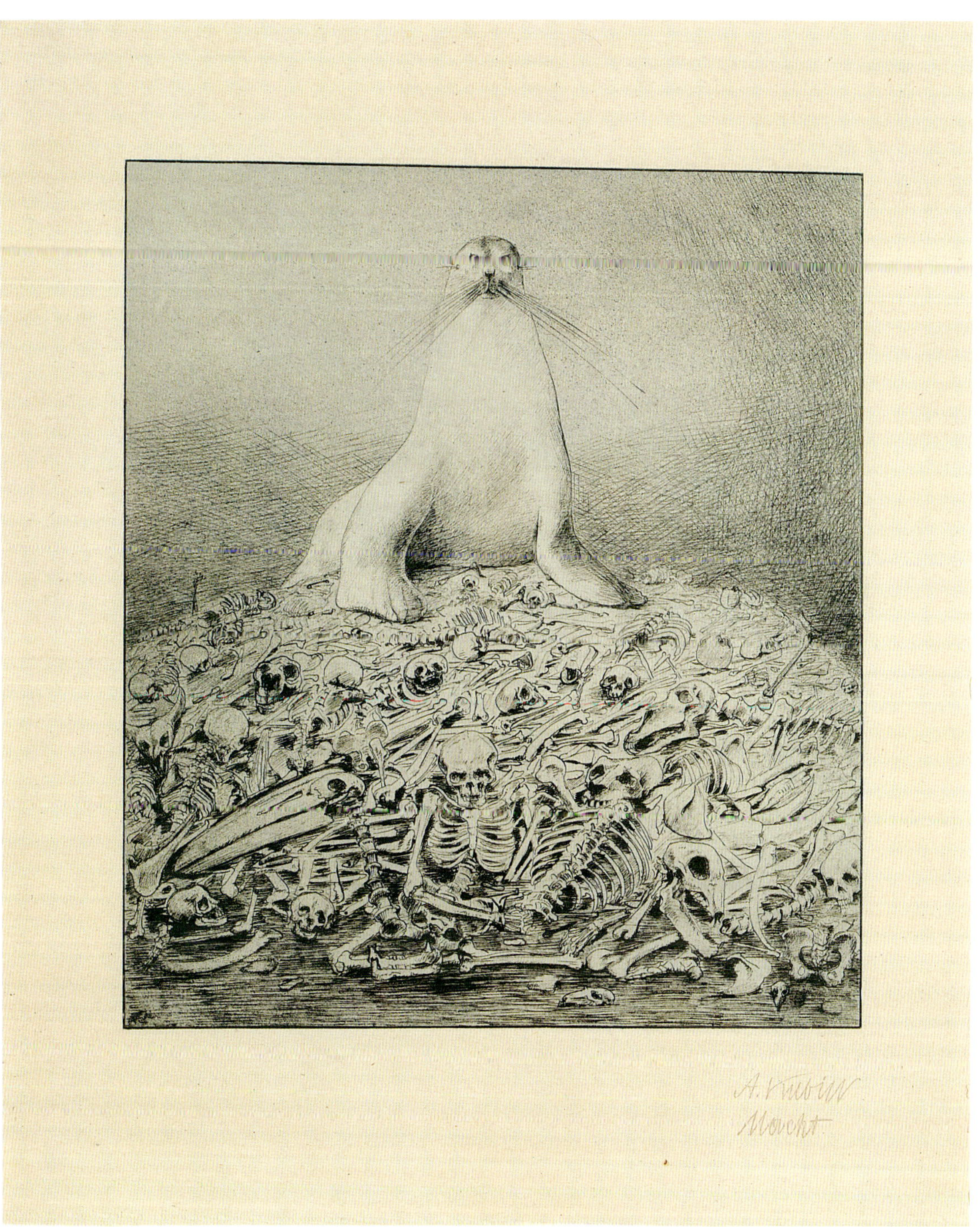

Cat. 42

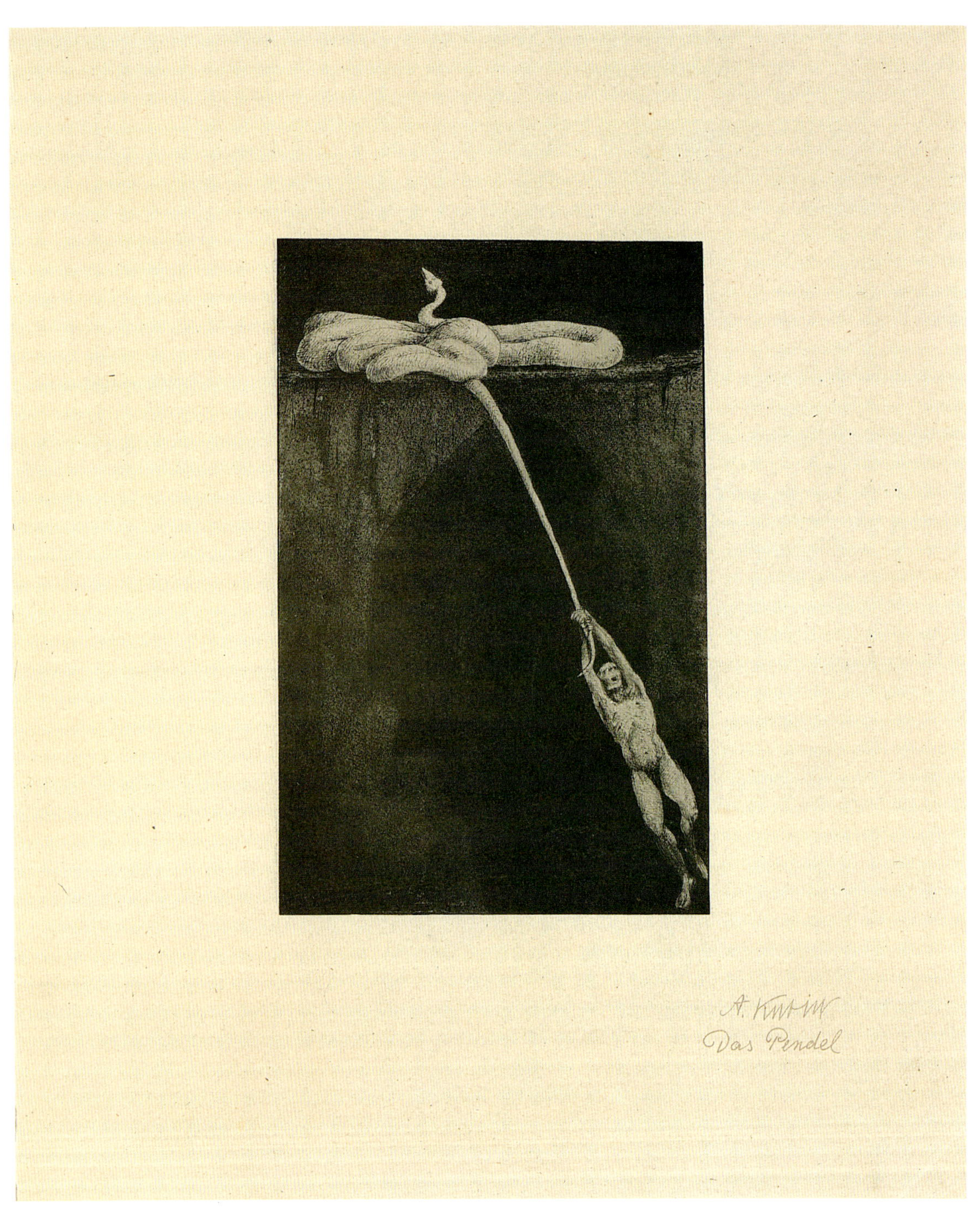

Cat. 43

78

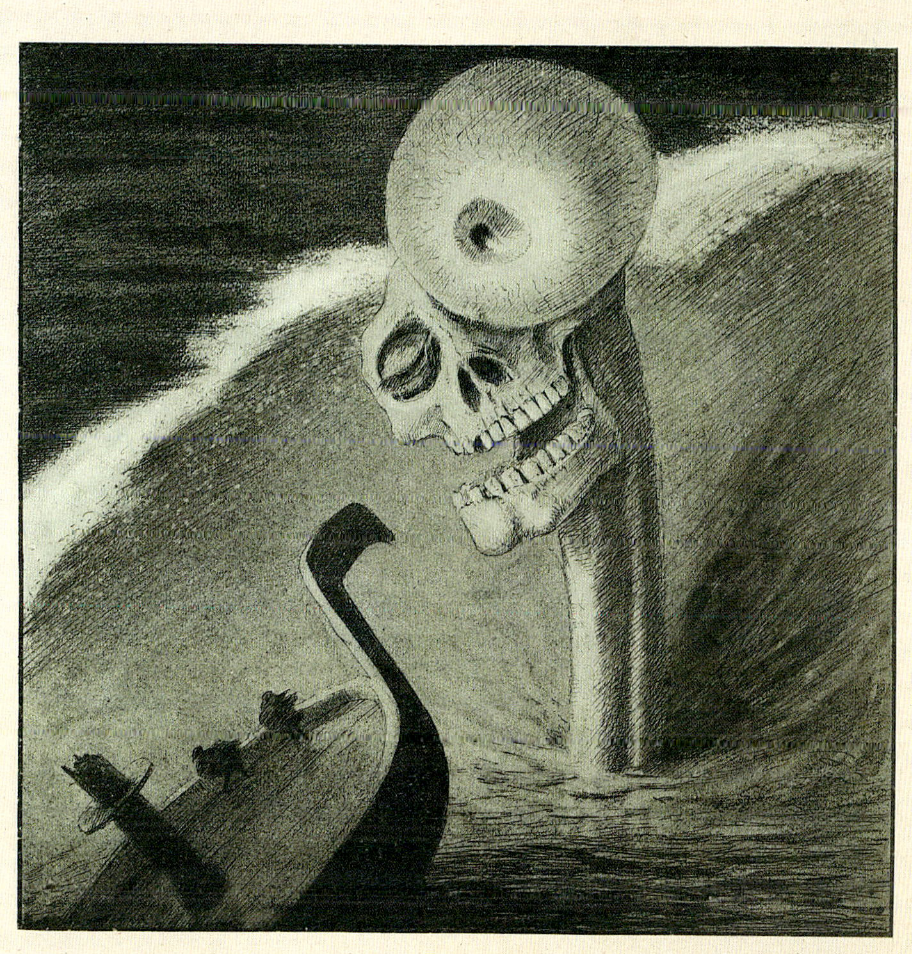

42

Alfred Kubin
Power, from the Weber Series, 1903
collotype, 55 x 40 cm
Inv.Nr. 791

43

Alfred Kubin
The Pendulum, from the Weber Series, 1903
collotype, 55 x 40 cm
Inv.Nr. 791

44

Alfred Kubin
The Horror, from the Weber Series, 1903
collotype, 55 x 40 cm
Inv.Nr. 791

45

Alfred Kubin
Pieta, 1915
lithograph, 44,2 x 32 cm
Inv.Nr. 76

46

Alfred Kubin
The Victor, 1928
lithograph, 45 x 34,3 cm
Inv.Nr. 1220

47

Alfred Kubin
Department Store, ca. 1925
collotype, 29 x 37,4 cm
Inv.Nr. 1277

48

Alfred Kubin
Breakfast at the Beach, ca. 1925
collotype, 28 x 37,8 cm
Inv.Nr. 1278

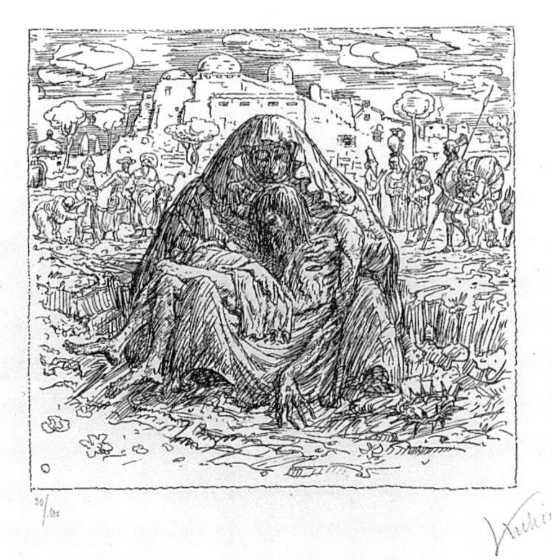

Cat. 45

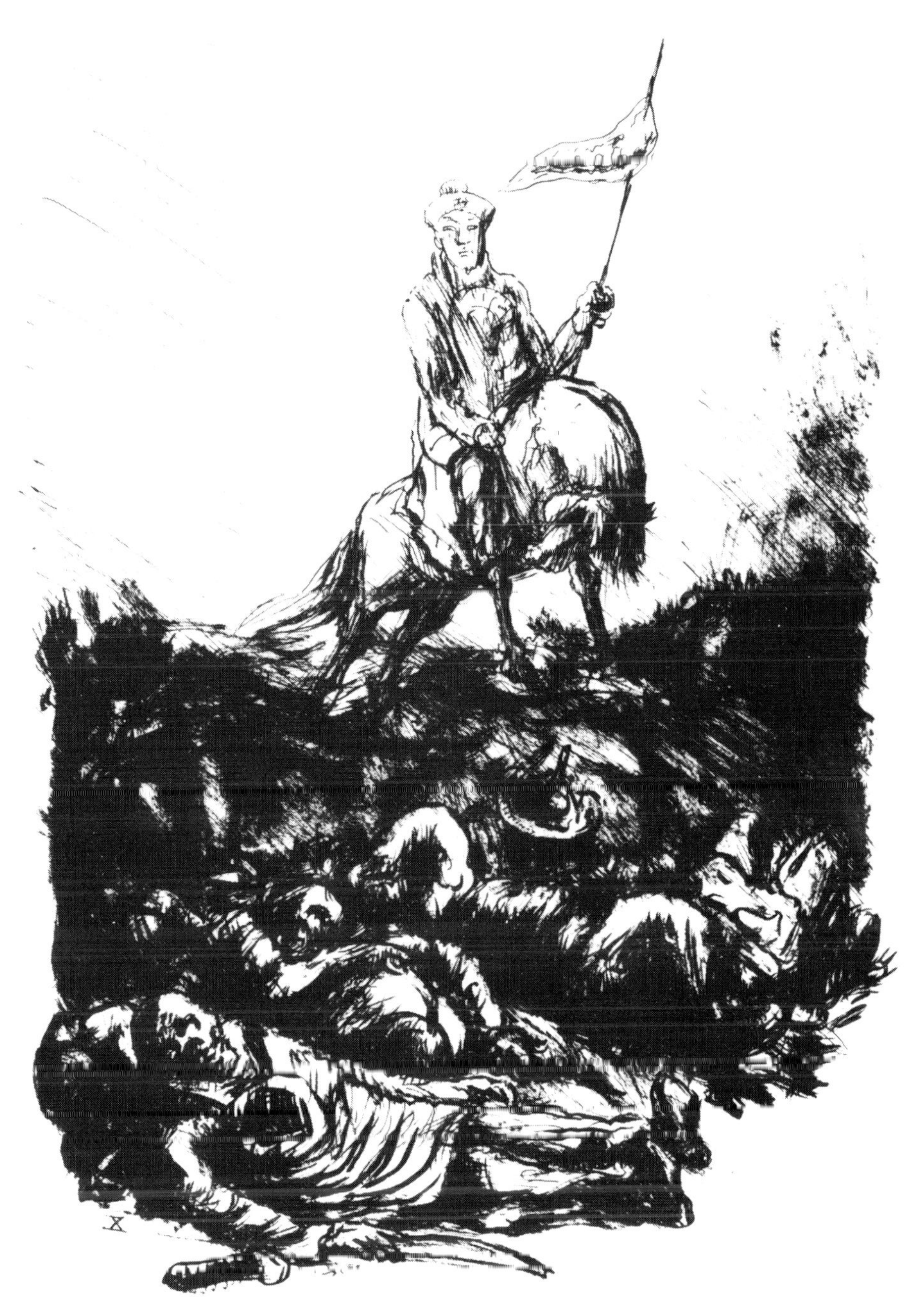

Cat. 46

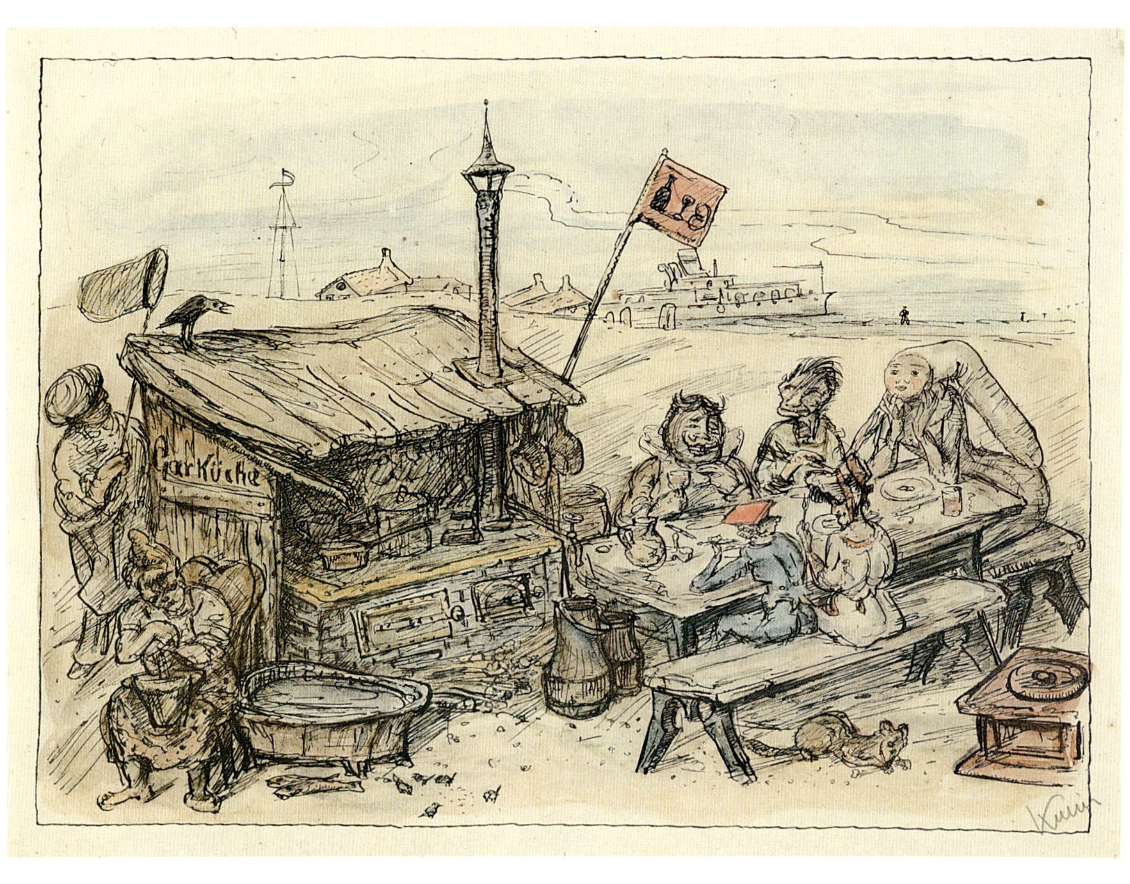

Cat. 48

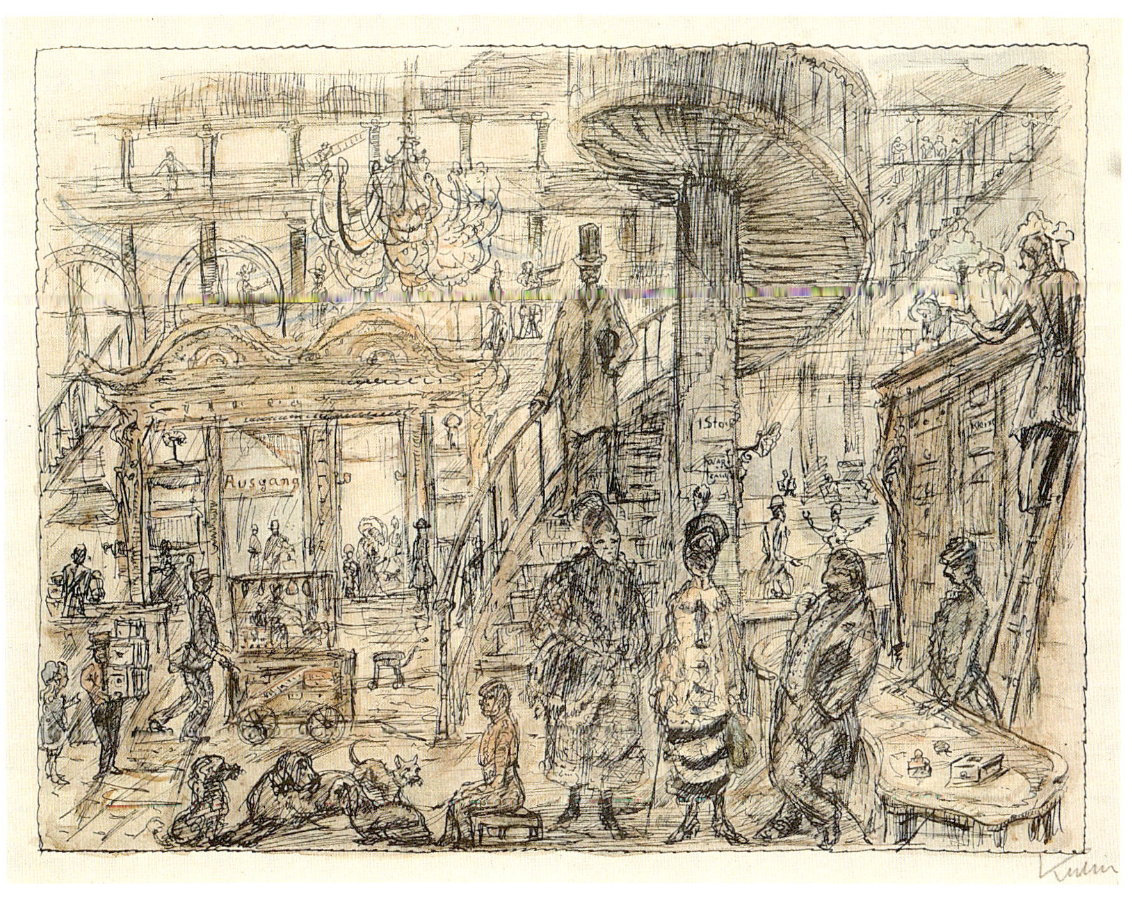

Cat. 47

Erwin Lang

Born Vienna, 22. 7. 1886
died Vienna, 10. 2. 1962
1903—07 studied applied arts at the Wiener Kunstgewerbeschule under Carl Otto Czeschka and Erich Mallina. Stage designer in Vienna and Berlin. 1908 exhibited his graphic art at the "Kunstschau". 1911 exhibited his paintings in a Sonderausstellung (special exhibition) of the Hagenbund organized by O. Kokoschka, E. Schiele, A. Faistauer, A. Kolig and Erwin Lang.
1920 return from Russian prisoner of war camp.
1925—38 member of the Hagenbund. After 1949 member of the Wiener Secession. 1914 received the Silberne Staatsmedaille and the medal of the Leipzig Booktrade Exhibition. 1933 Price of the City of Vienna, 1934 Award of the Republic of Austria (Staatspreis).
Erwin Lang was married to the dancer Grete Wiesenthal. He created stage settings and posters for her. Numerous book illustrations. The art of the woodcut was his field of specialization. Radical simplification of line and magnificent light effects characterize his work.

49
Erwin Lang
from the portfolio Grete Wiesenthal, Dance Album, 1911
woodcut on paper, 46,5 x 35 cm
Inv.Nr. 4920

50
Erwin Lang
from the portfolio Grete Wiesenthal, Dance Album, 1911
woodcut on paper, 46,5 x 35 cm
Inv.Nr. 4921

51
Erwin Lang
Boy, from Dante's Vita Nuova, 1913
woodcut on paper, 46 x 37,5 cm
Inv.Nr. 4923

52
Erwin Lang
Sitting Half-Nude, from Dante's Vita Nuova, 1913
woodcut on paper, 46 x 37,5 cm
Inv.Nr. 4924

Cat. 51

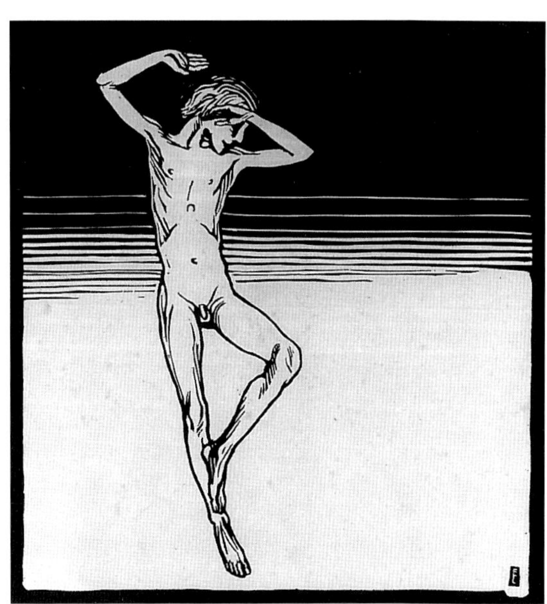

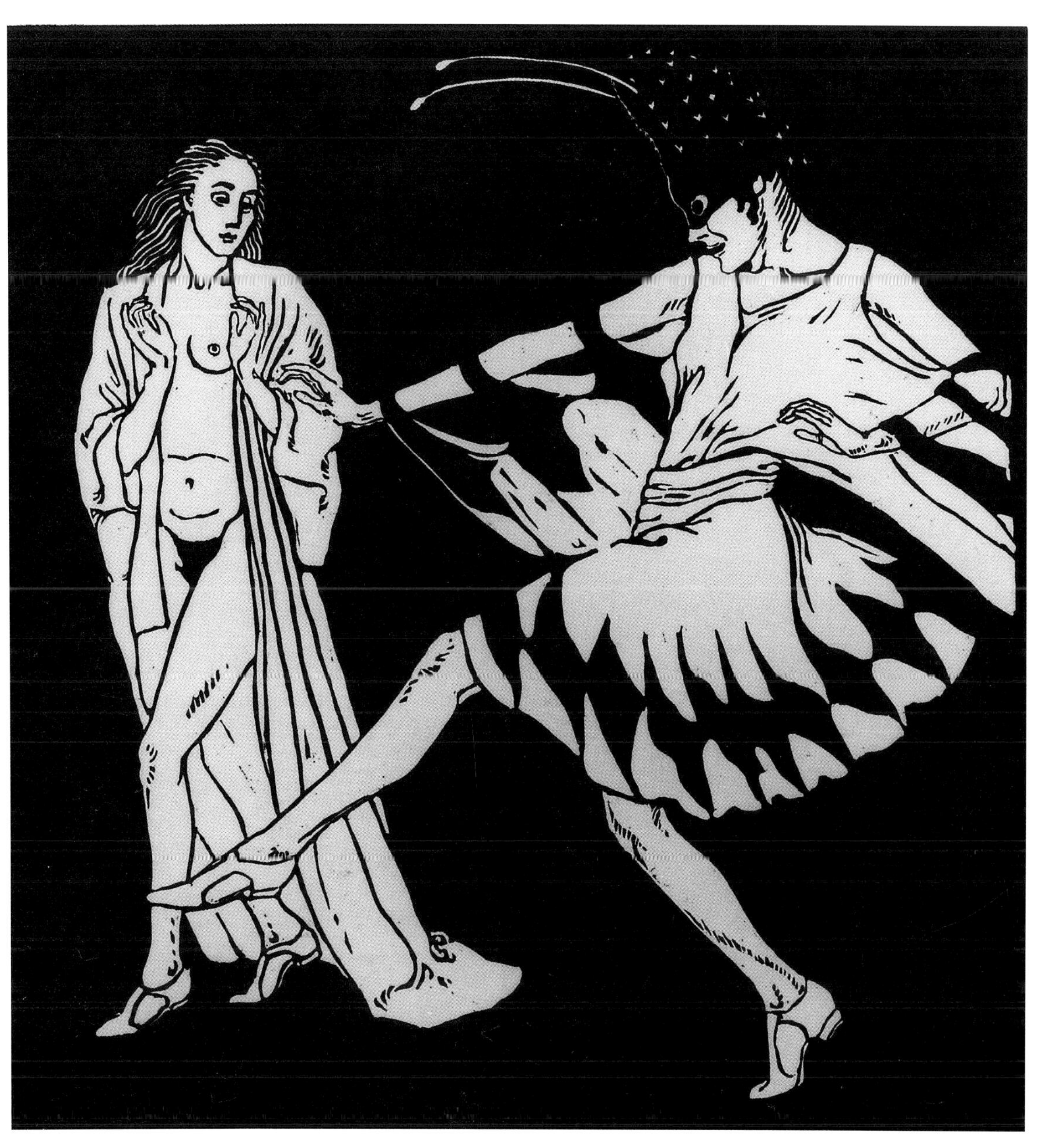

Cat. 50

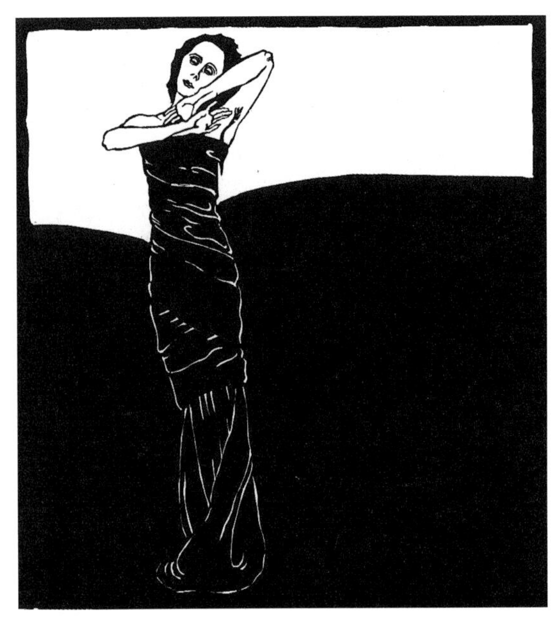

Cat. 49

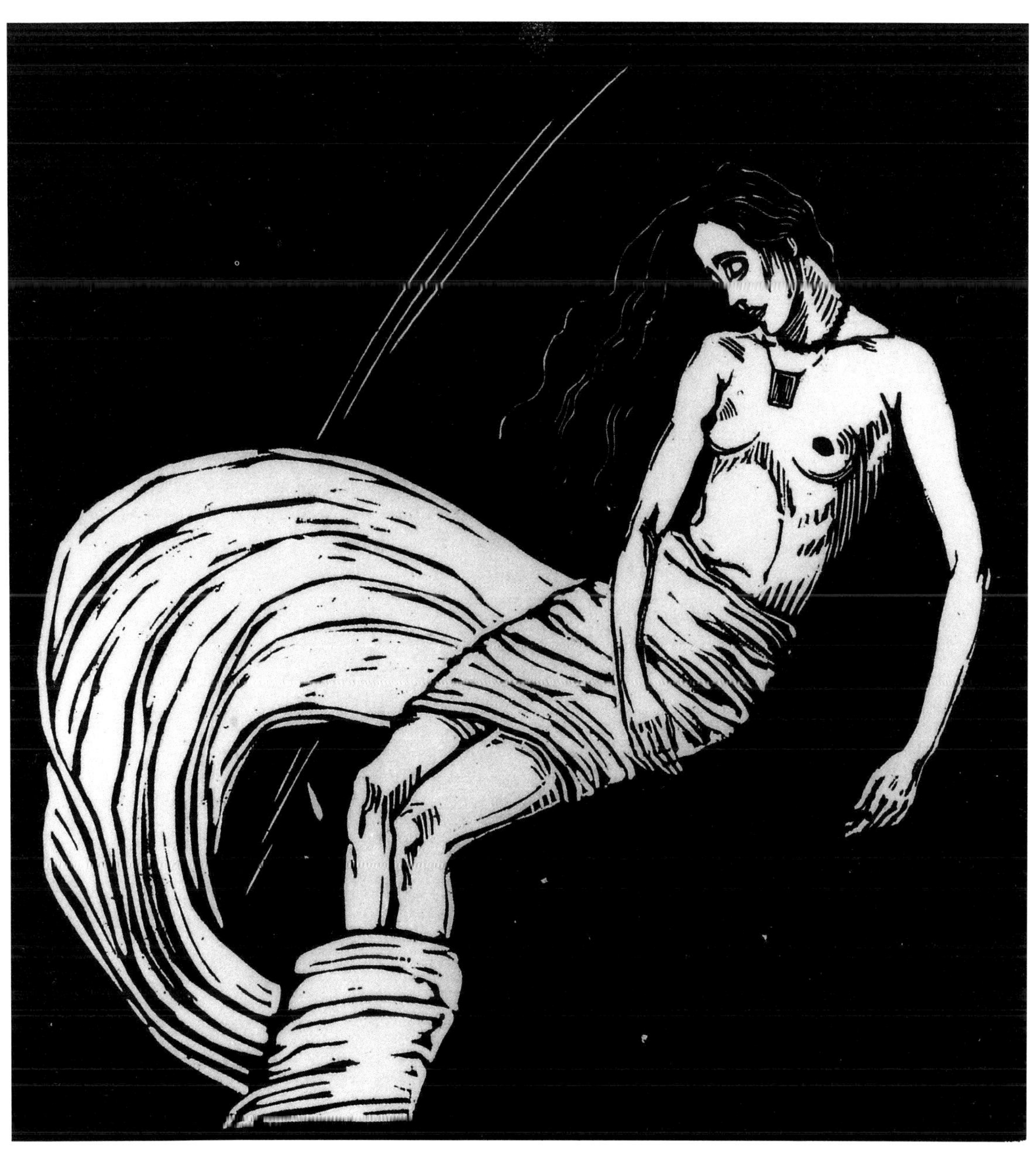

Oskar Laske

Born Czernowitz, 8. 1. 1874
died Vienna, 30. 11. 1951
After attending the Realschule in Vienna, he studied painting privately with the landscape painter Anton Hlavaček during 1888/89. 1892—98 studied at the Technische Hochschule (technical university) in Vienna, mainly with Karl König, then from 1899—1901 with Otto Wagner at the Akademie der bildenden Künste (fine arts). The following years he worked in the studio of his father, later on he worked on his own (mosaic facade of the "Engelsapotheke", etc.). Designed the cabaret "Nachtlicht". In addition to architectural commissions, he did drawings and water-colors in the style of the Secession. 1904 first attempts at engravings: content and style similar to the caricatures of the humorous magazines "Simplicissimus" and "Der liebe Augustin". 1904—05 travel to England and Scotland, then participation in the exhibition of the Jungbund on the premises of the Hagenbund. He exhibited landscapes, cityscapes and folklore — the results of his various trips and themes to which he adhered also later in his life. Then Laske turned exclusively to painting; he became a member of the Hagenbund and developed his decorative, flat style. Stylisized structure interested Laske more than genre and content.
Human figures, animals and plants serve as compositional elements for a stylistic method which tends to lose exactness. The stylization of so many of his art works is reminiscent of compositional principles embraced by the Secession artists; but Laske did not take the step towards abstraction.
Before the outbreak of World War One Laske traveled throughout Europe and to Tunesia. His repeated preoccupation with religious topics resulted in the 1919 commission of a "Noah's ark" frieze for the war orphanage in Kalksburg, Lower Austria. In the same year, he published the "Faust-Impressionen", a portfolio of nine engravings reflecting in part his own war experience. 1920 his first stage design: Shakespeare, "Much Ado About Nothing". Journeys, exhibitions, awards, and honorary memberships accompanied his further career and work. He adhered to the secessionist-impressionist principles all his life.

53
Oskar Laske
The Common Path to Noah, 1912
etching, 36 x 45 to 40 x 52 cm
Inv.Nr. 2608

54
Oskar Laske
The Anchorites, 1920
etching, 29,5 x 27,5 cm
Inv.Nr. 2508

55
Oskar Laske
Absalom, My Son, 1929
drypoint etching with aquatint and aquarelle,
15 x 13,5 to 28,7 x 25,1 cm
Inv.Nr. 3641

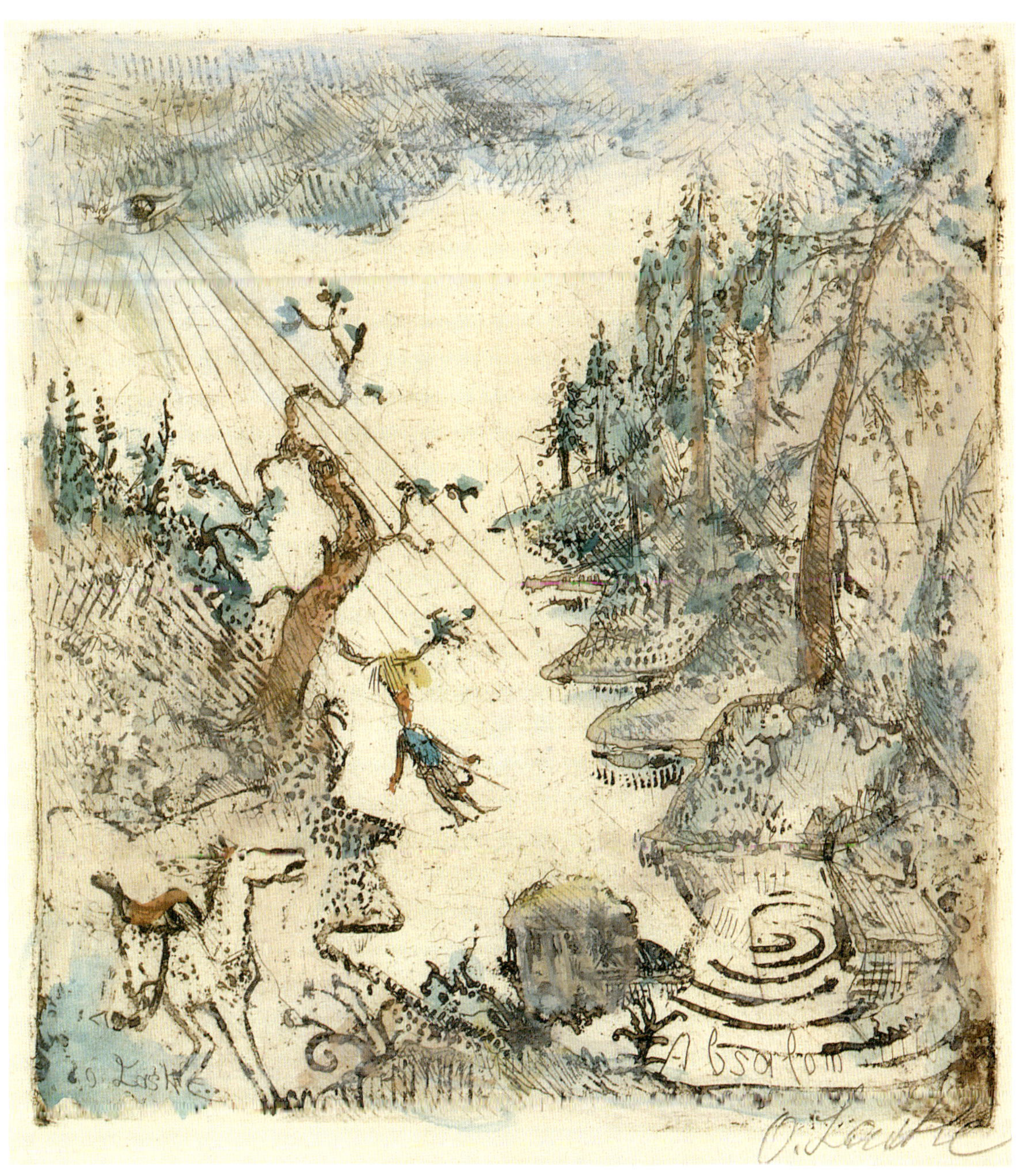

Absalom

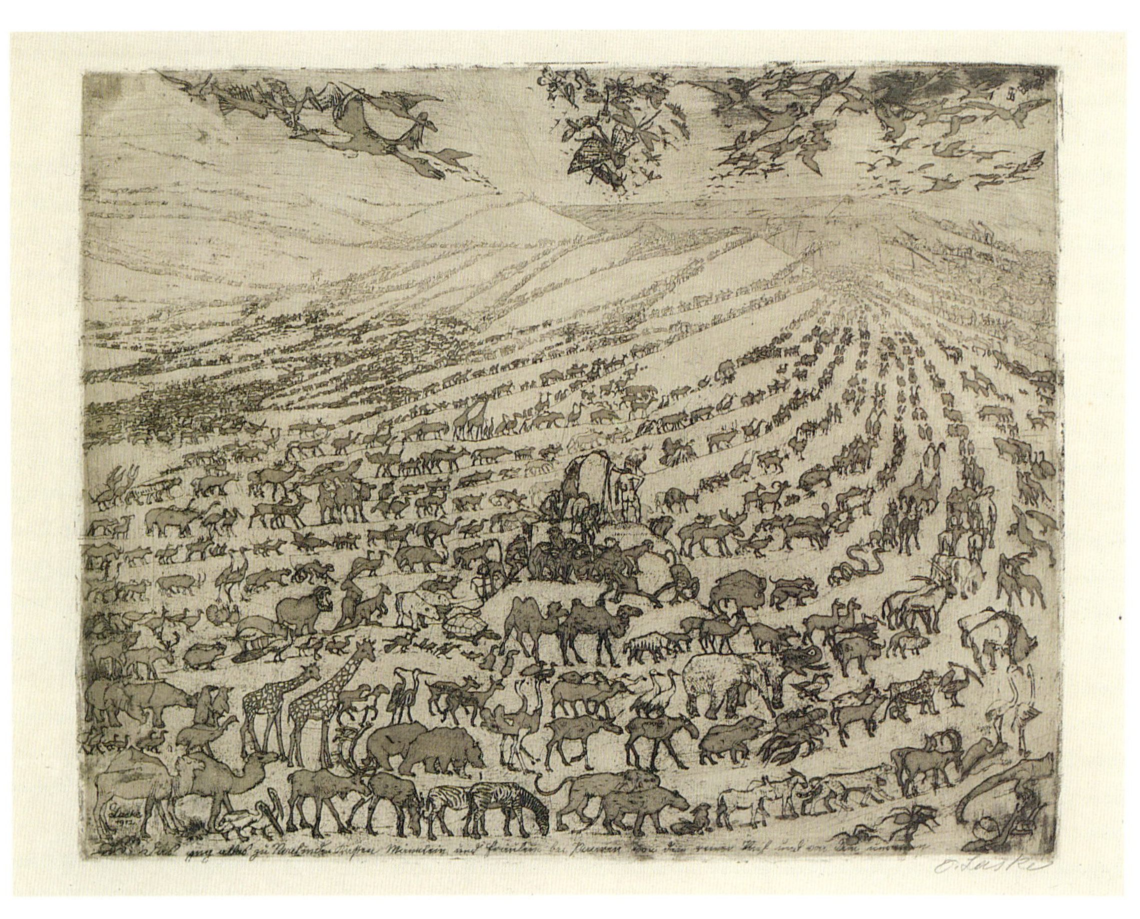

Cat. 53

90

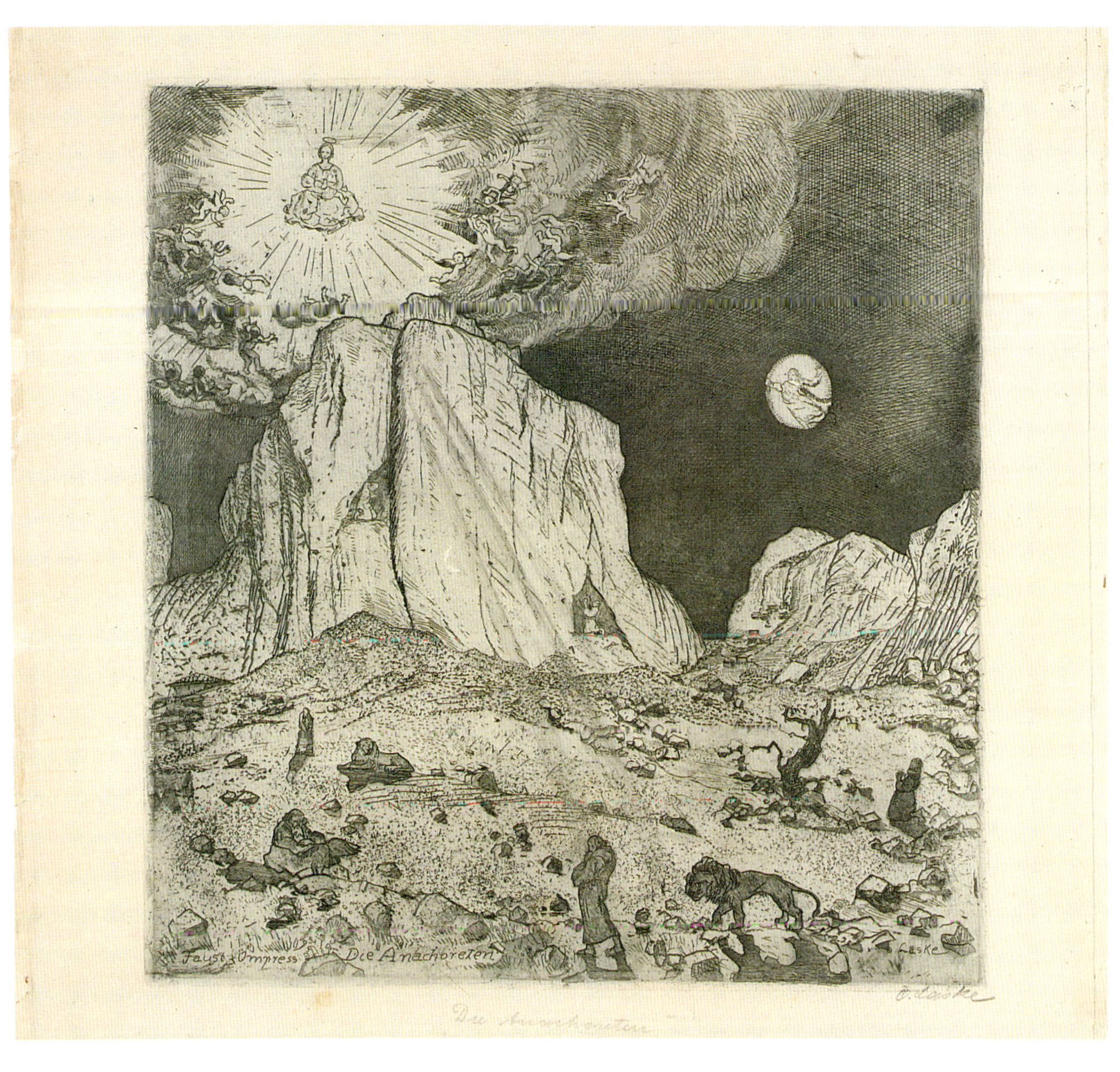

Cat. 54

Berthold Löffler

Born Nieder-Rosenthal bei Reichenberg, Bohemia,
28. 9. 1874
died Vienna, 23. 3. 1960
Löffler believed to have inherited his propensity for
drawing from his father who designed cloth patterns
for his textile store (from Löffler, "Von meinem
Werden"). His mother supported his plan to become
a painter. Löffler visited the drawing-school of the
Gewerbemuseum (Museum of Crafts) in his native
Reichenberg in 1890. He enrolled at the
Kunstgewerbeschule (applied arts) in Vienna where
he studied with Franz Matsch and Carl Otto
Czeschka. As a student, he designed the cover of a
satirical version of the "Ver Sacrum" called "Quer
Sacrum — Organ der Vereinigung bildender Künstler
Irrlands" (published in 1899). 1900 termination of his
studies under Kolo Moser, studied fresco technique
with Andreas Groll. Contributed to the frescos in the
vault of the St. Brigitta Chapel; active as illustrator
(Gerlach, "Allegorien", "Des Knaben Wunderhorn").
1907 teacher at the Kunstgewerbeschule and one
year later co-founder of the "Kunstschau" and
"Werkbund". Co-founder with Michael Powolny and
the sculptor Lang of the Wiener Keramik. Initially its
products were rejected by the Viennese, but a set of
four season-figures designed by Löffler met with
success followed by business contacts with the
Wiener Werkstätte in 1907. 1904—05 tile-room for the
cabaret "Fledermaus"; worked at the Sanatorium
Purkersdorf. 1905—11 tiles for the Palais Stoclet in
Brussels.
At the Werkbundausstellung 1912 in the Öster-
reichisches Museum für Kunst und Industrie the
Wiener Keramik had its own room decorated by
Löffler's wall-paper; its novelty was black-white
ceramics.
Due to mounting financial difficulties, the Wiener
Keramik hat to be sold to the Gmundner Keramik.
1911 final exhibition.
1912 series of pictures and a tiled room for the
Salzburger Volkskeller of the Hotel Pittner. 1913
interior decoration of a Ringstraßen-Café and the
Stadtkeller in St. Pölten, Lower Austria. 1915—18
military service. After the war, publication of color
lithographs for the "Amoretten" calendar of the Wiener
Werkstätte. 1922 member of the Künstlerhaus which
published the booklet "Die vier Temperamente" (The
Four Temperaments) with Löffler's illustrations. Works
of the thirties: war memorial in Trautmannsdorf, St.
Christopher in Dürnstein, various works in Kirchberg
am Wechsel.

56
Berthold Löffler
The Bird Catcher
lead and colored pencil on paper,
22,8 x 31,5 cm
Dr. Czerny Donation
Inv.Nr. 3370

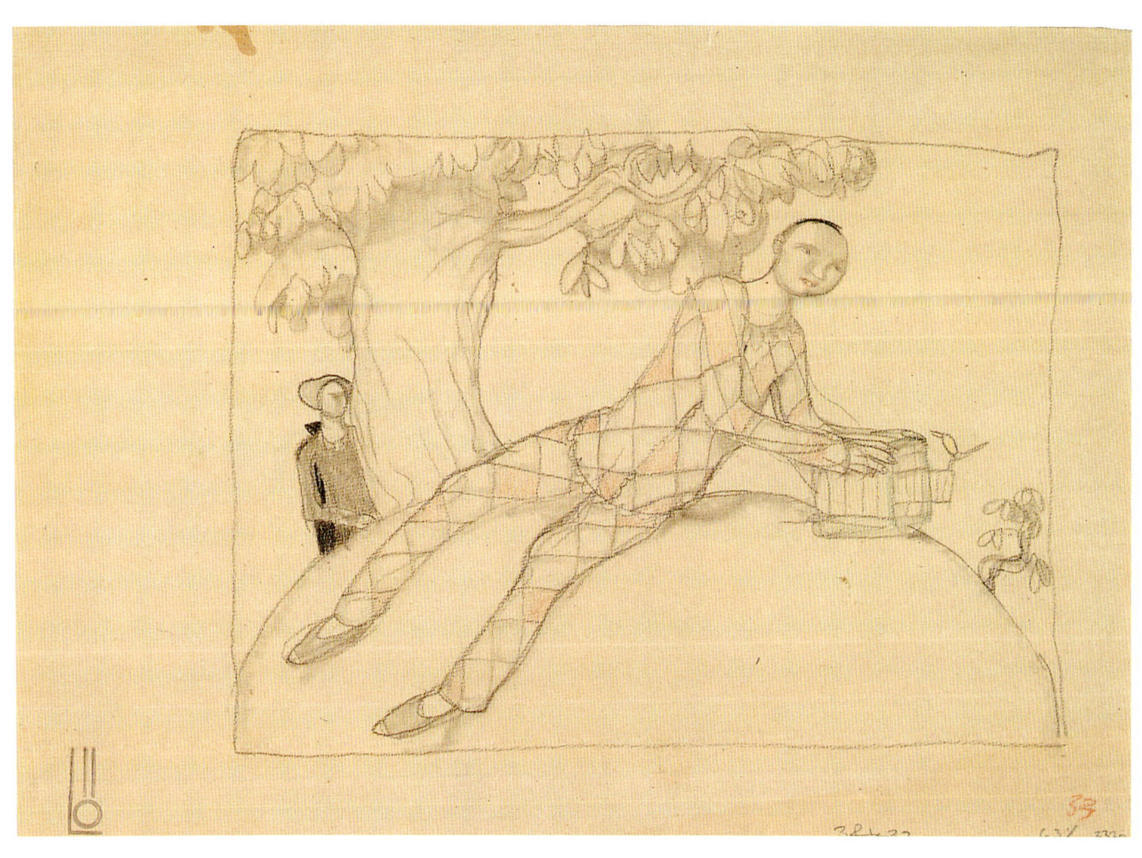

Cat. 56

Max Oppenheimer (Mopp)

Born Vienna, 1885
died New York, 1954
Son of the writer Ludwig Oppenheimer. Enrolled at the Vienna Academy at the age of fifteen. 1903—06 studied at the Academy in Prague. 1908 exhibited at the Vienna "Kunstschau", returned shortly thereafter to Vienna and joined the artists associated with E. Schiele and A. P. Gütersloh. Painted many portraits of well-known writers and musicians during these years in Vienna. 1911 moved to Berlin, sponsored by the art dealer Paul Cassirer. 1915 moved to Switzerland. 1924/25 back in Vienna; fall of 1924 exhibited 200 art works in the Hagenbund rooms. 1926—38 lived again in Berlin. Fled from the Nazis and took refuge in Switzerland. 1938 autobiographical book "Menschen finden ihren Maler" (People Find Their Painter), published in Zurich. 1939 left Switzerland for New York where he lived for the rest of his life.
In 1940 Gallery Kallir-Nirenstein, New York, whose manager previously ran the Neue Galerie in Vienna, organized an exhibition with paintings such as "Tilla Durieux, Geißelung" (Flagellation), and "Der Weltkrieg" (the world war). These paintings of his early period are representative of Viennese expressionism with its exaggerated pictorial representation, dynamic coloring and extreme perspective.
MOPP soon tried to harness these inspirations and strike a balance between graphic and painterly representation. From 1912 cubist elements are significant components of his compositions.
Apart from music, an early element in his work (being an ambitious violinist himself), MOPP's main attention turned to portraiture, as exemplified by paintings of Thomas and Heinrich Mann, Peter Altenberg, Arthur Schnitzler, Arnold Schönberg, all done before the beginning of World War One.
In his later years he favored still lifes, above all small things of everyday life; here he comes close to the threshold of abstraction.

57

Max Oppenheimer
The Rosé Quartett, 1925
etching, 22,3 x 22,7 to 35 x 27,5 cm
Inv.Nr. 1758

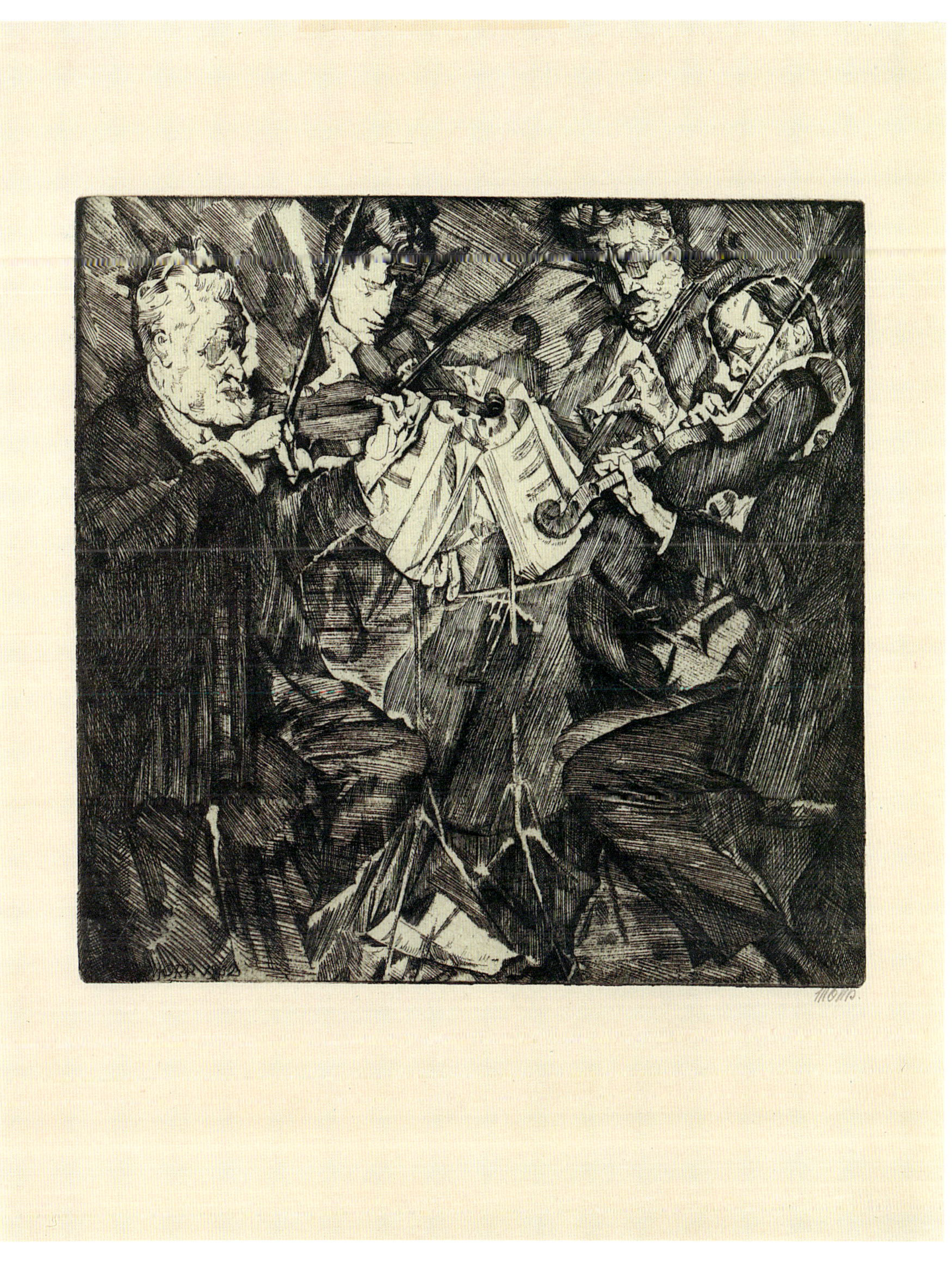

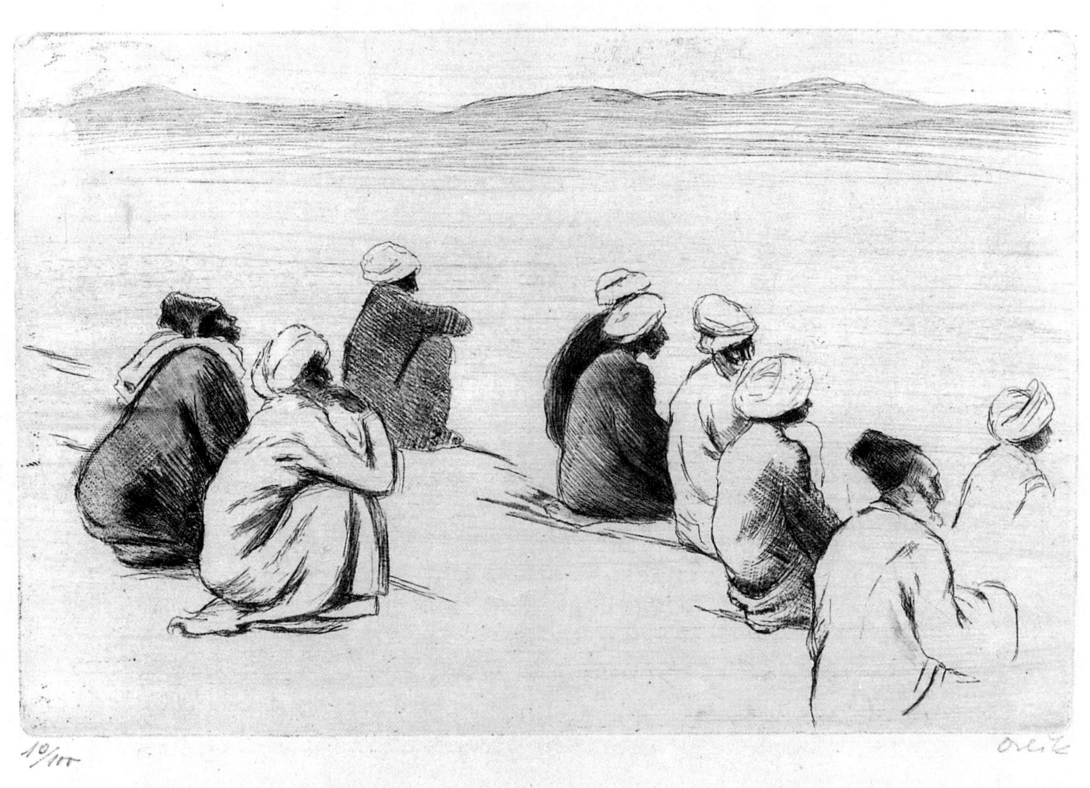

Emil Orlik

Born Prague, 21. 7. 1870
died Berlin, 28. 9. 1932
Studied at the Munich Academy with H. Knirr, W. Lindenschmidt and J. L. Raab. 1898 went to Holland, Belgium, England, Scotland and then to Paris. Circa 1900 first trip to Japan which was decisive in his stylistic development. His own woodcuts of this period show the adoption of Japanese elements. In 1911 he visited Japan as well as China, India, and Egypt. Orlik was considered a "rejuvenator of modern color woodcut". His delicate coloring stood for a "Japanese sensibility".
His first Vienna exhibition in 1902 met with great success. Ludwig Hevesi ("Österreichische Kunst 1848—1900", 1903) called him a "graphic talent" and with Orlik's work in mind used the Japanese word "omoshiroi" which means interesting, amusing, genial.
Orlik was a popular character in Berlin; at concerts and plays he used to draw a "gallery of contemporaries" on slips of paper and place-cards.

His engravings of famous persons such as G. Hauptmann (1909), G. Mahler (1903), Bach (1915), Michelangelo (1913), Schopenhauer (1922), and R. Strauss (1917) impressed their viewers: examples of Orlik's masterly skills combined with psychological insight.

58

Emil Orlik
Spectators at the Camel Races, 1912
etching on hand-made paper with deckle edge, 13 x 20 to 20 x 26 cm
Inv.Nr. 1373

59

Emil Orlik
Beethoven Concert, 1922
etching on hand-made paper with deckle edge, 13 x 20 to 20 x 26 cm
Inv.Nr. 1374

96

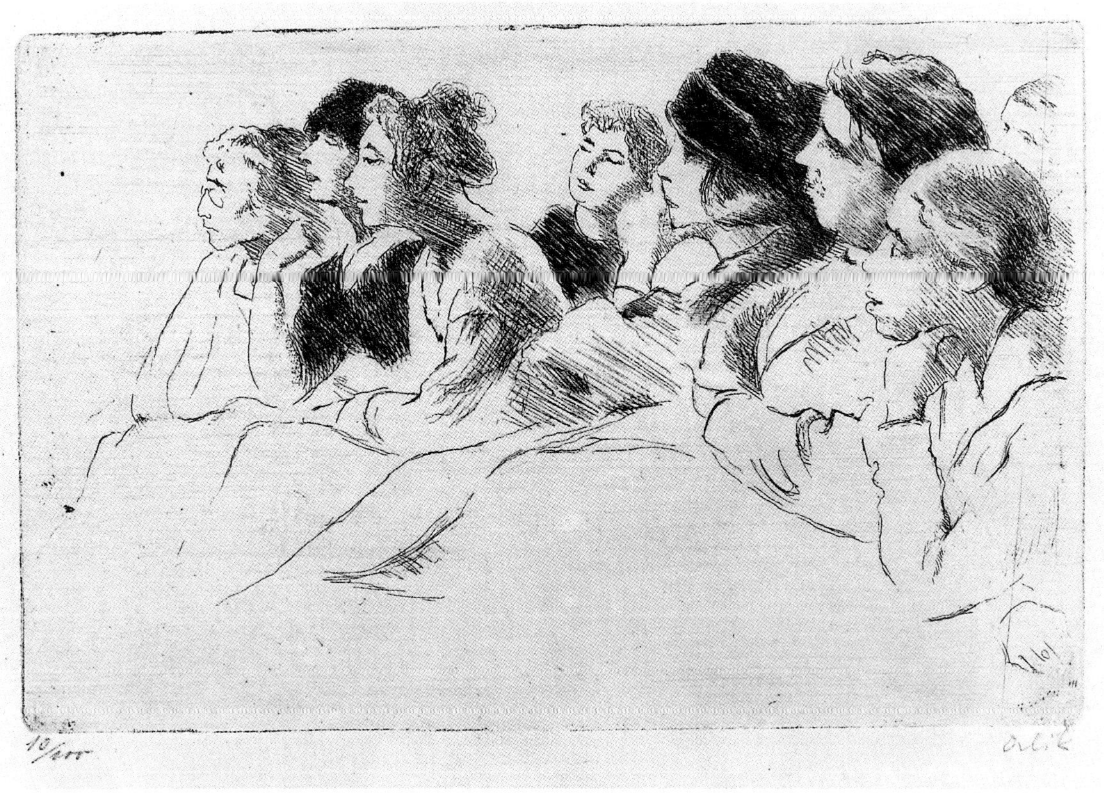

Cat. 59

Carl Anton Reichel

Born Wels, Upper Austria, 1874
died Vienna, 1944
Descendant of an old Franconian-Bavarian family. Attended Gymnasium in Salzburg and Kremsmünster, studied medicine in Vienna, Prague and Munich. In his early twenties extensive interest in psychiatry, psychology, art history, and indology. 1900 in Paris which left a strong imprint upon his career as a graphic artist. Woodcuts, then a corpus of about 300 engravings which met with considerable success. They were neglected for decades and rediscovered in the wake of a 1970 Albertina exhibition, Vienna.
1905 first marriage with Russian aristocrat. Lived in Großgmain near Salzburg, then for ten years with Hermann Bahr in Castle Bürgelstein. Reichel acted as artistic and private advisor of high-ranking personalities such as Crown Prince Rupprecht von Bayern. Friend of the composers Hans Pfitzner, Arnold Schönberg as well as Alfred Kubin who owned many Reichel engravings. 1917 purchased the Edelhof in Micheldorf, Upper Austria, which was until 1924 an artistic, intellectual and political center. 1933 left for Switzerland, returned to Austria and spent his last years in Vienna in company of his second wife, the Burgtheater actress Tony van Eyck.
Reichel the graphic artist was basically an autodidact. He made portraits and nudes in the fashionable tradition of modern French artists; the core of his oeuvre, however, are those unique and incomparable drawings that combine Art Nouveau elements with highly abstracted figures in dramatic, frequently visionary representations. Reichel's penchant for Buddhism, psychic marginal states, music (G. Mahler), and literature enters into these creations as do his extraordinary sensitivity for formal processes and tones as well as vibrations peculiar to engravings.

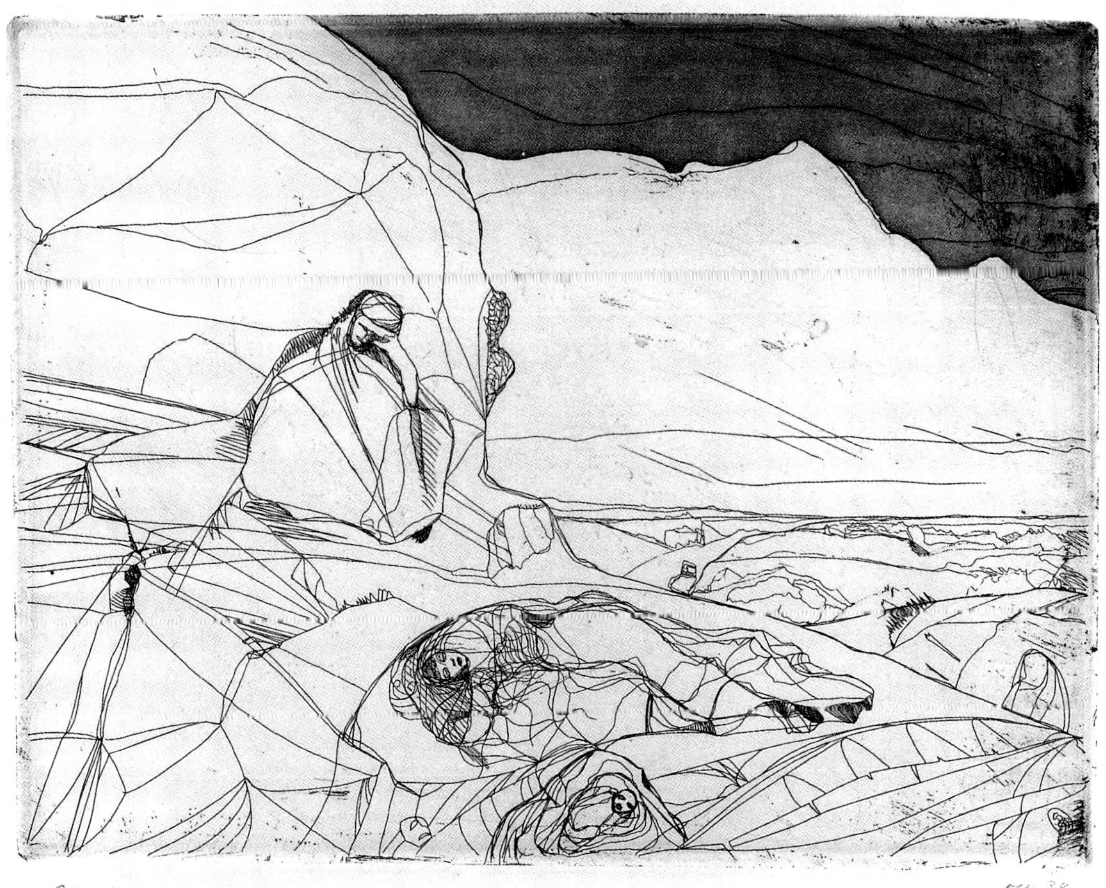

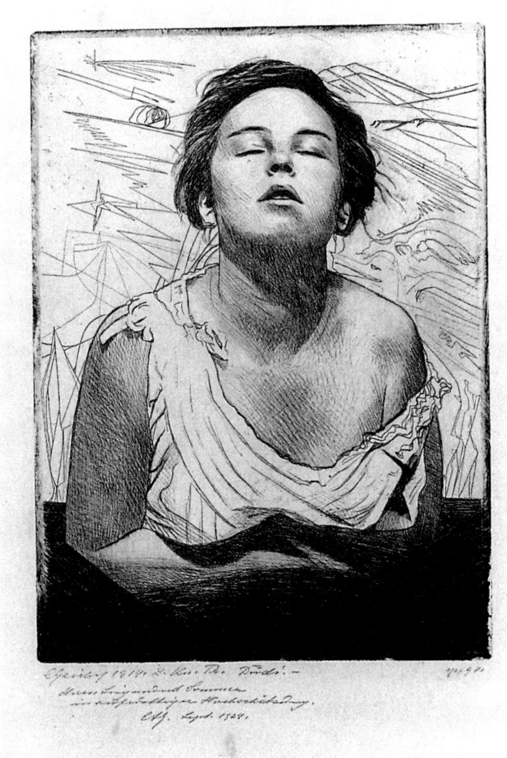

Cat. 61

60

Carl Anton Reichel
Elegy, Opus 34, 1913
etching, 22,5 x 28,5 to 31,5 x 38,5 cm
Inv.Nr. CAR

61

Carl Anton Reichel
Portrait of a Girl, Dudi, 1914
etching, 32,2 x 23,6 to 47,5 x 31 cm
Inv.Nr. 2226

62

Carl Anton Reichel
Gods, Opus 256, 1918
etching, 26,5 x 20 to 40 x 25 cm
Inv.Nr. 1918

63

Carl Anton Reichel
Opus 242, 1918
etching, 22 x 28,5 to 26 x 41 cm
Inv.Nr. CAR

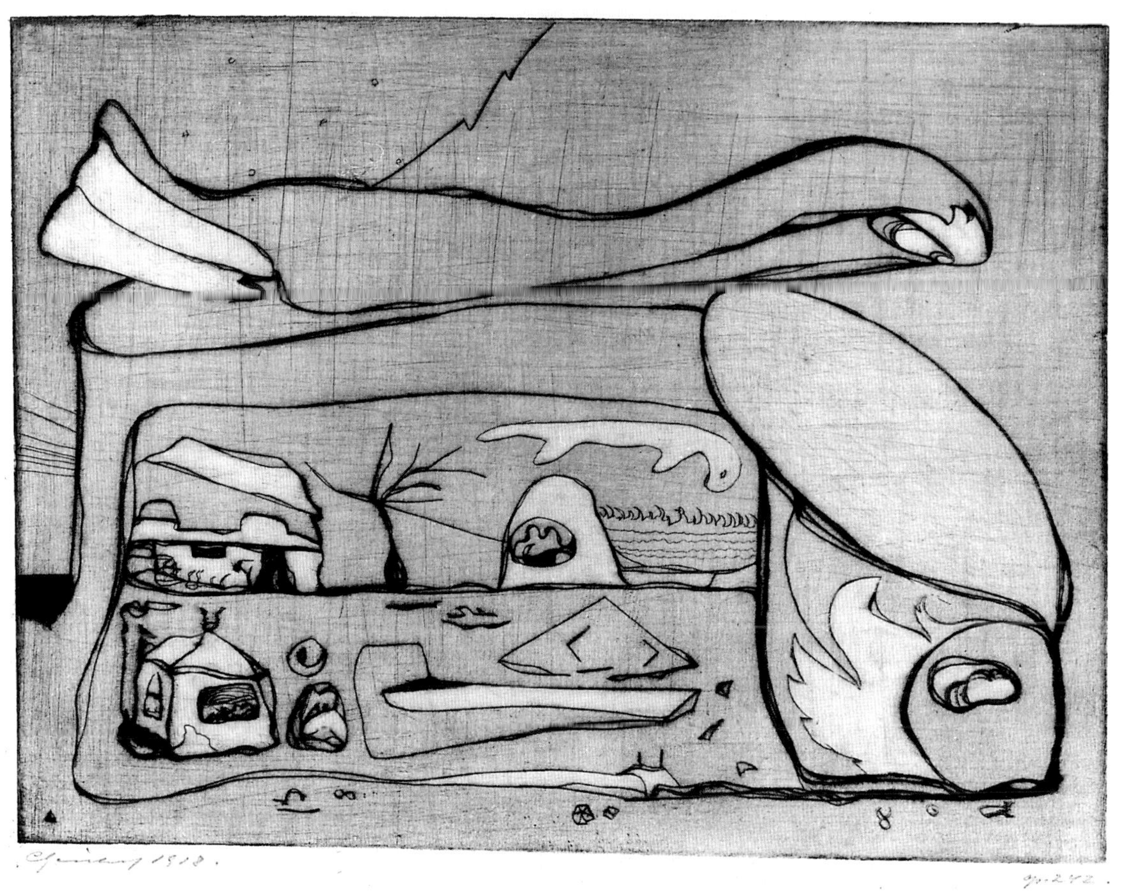

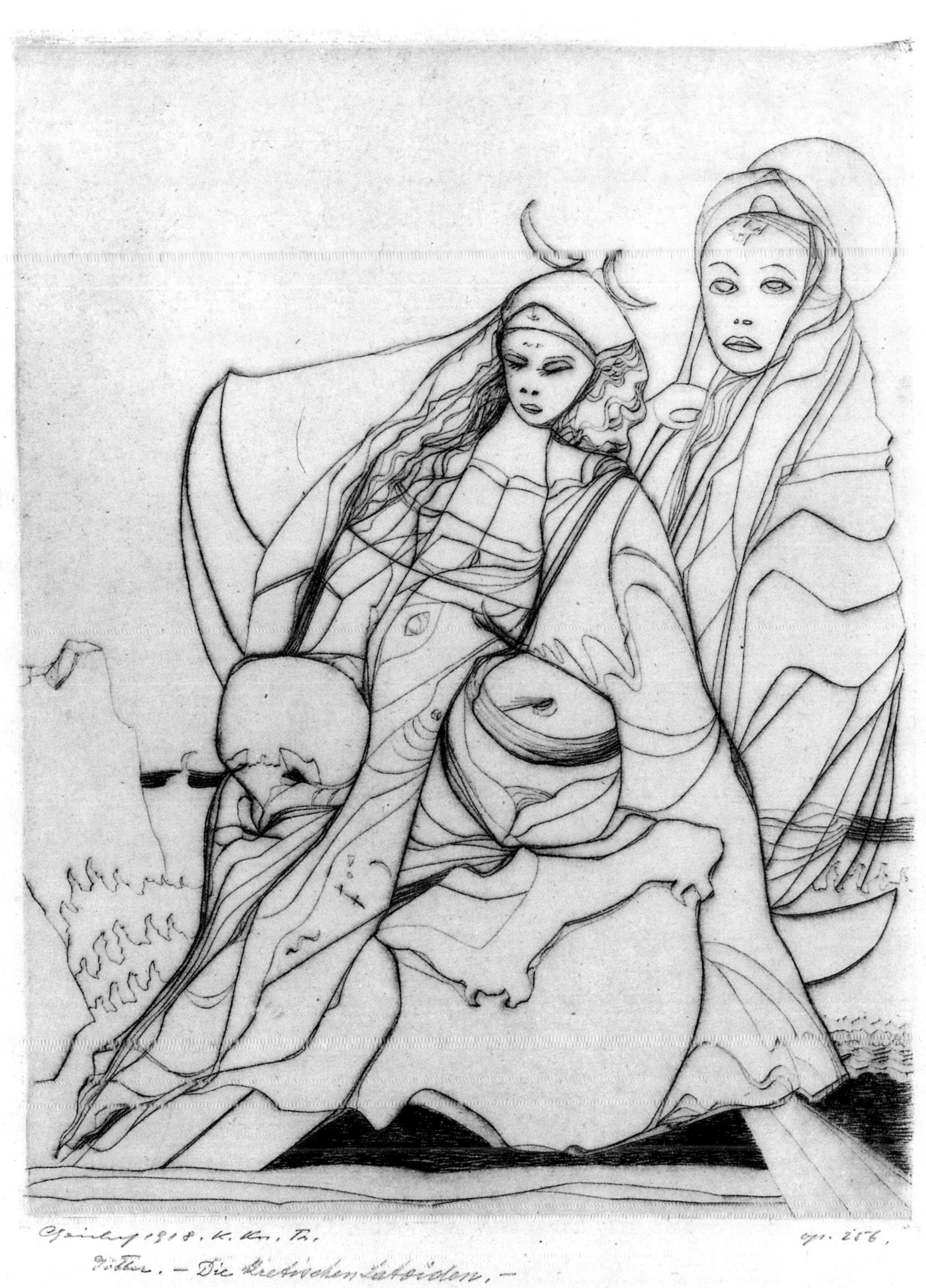

Egon Schiele

1890 Born on 12th June in Tulln on the Danube, Austria.

1902 After attending elementary school in Tulln and one term at the high school in Krems, Schiele attends the high school in Klosterneuburg.

1905 The father dies. Schiele's godfather and uncle Leopold Czihaczek is appointed guardian.

1906 Schiele's teachers recommend an artistic education. In autumn, he begins to attend the Academy of Fine Arts in Vienna, taking lectures given by Professor Christian Griepenkerl (1839—1916).

1907 Schiele establishes his first own artist's studio in Vienna. Personal acquaintance with Gustav Klimt.

1908 First participation in a public exhibition.

1909 Leaves the Academy in April. Foundation of the „Neukunstgruppe" (Group for New Art) together with like-minded artists. Exhibits four pictures at the "Internationale Kunstschau" in Vienna (1909). Contacts with Josef Hoffmann and the "Wiener Werkstätte" (Vienna Workshop). In December, the "Neukunstgruppe" exhibits for the first time in the Pisko Gallery at Schwarzenbergplatz.

1910 Through the intercession of Josef Hoffmann, Schiele can exhibit a picture at the "International Hunting Exhibition" in Vienna. At the exhibition in Klosterneuburg, Schiele gets acquainted with the government official and art collector Heinrich Benesch.

1911 First collective exhibition in the Miethke Gallery in Vienna (April—May). Studio in Krumau, home town of his mother. Lives together with the model Wally Neuzil. In August, relocation to Neulengbach. Contacts to the Munich art dealer Hans Goltz. In November, Schiele becomes a member of the artists' association "Sema" in Munich.

1912 Exhibition together with the "Neukunstgruppe" in Budapest. The Goltz Gallery in Munich shows works of Schiele along with others done by members of the artists' association "Der Blaue Reiter". Exhibition in the Folkwang Museum in Hagen. With the "Sema Portfolio", Schiele's first lithograph appears, a self portrait as a nude. On 15th April, he is arrested in Neulengbach and later transferred to St. Pölten, where he is sentenced to three days investigative detention on the charge of having distributed indecent drawings. Participates in the "Hagenbund" exhibition. At the "Sonderbund" exhibition in Köln, Schiele shows three of his works. In October, the artist moves into a new studio in Vienna.

1913 Schiele becomes a member of the "Association of Austrian Artists" (Bund österreichischer Künstler) and participates in its exhibition in Budapest. Collective exhibition: at the Goltz Gallery in Munich as well as in other German cities.

1914 Exhibition "Konkurrenz C. R. — Paintings" at Pisko Gallery. In addition to the German-speaking region, Schiele participates in exhibitions in Rome, Brussels and Paris. As a result of his studying the art of graphic prints, six etchings are produced. The photographer Anton Josef Trčka takes several very expressive portrait photographs of Schiele.

1915 Exhibition of some of Schiele's œuvre in the Museum of Fine Arts in Zurich. Marriage with Edith Harms, conscripted into military service and called to Prague, returns to Vienna.

1916 Participates, inter alia, in exhibitions at the Berlin Secession within a programme of the "Wiener Kunstschau". Keeps a war diary. He ist delegated to the prisoner camp for officers, where he works in the chancellery administrating war supplies. He is provided with a studio and the opportunity to be active as an artist.

1917 Schiele is assigned to the Military Museum in Vienna. Participates in the war exhibition in the Kaisergarten (Prater) as well as in exhibitions of Austrian art in Amsterdam, Stockholm and Copenhagen.

1918 On 6th February, Gustav Klimt dies. At the 49th exhibition of the "Vienna Secession" in March, the main exhibition room is put at the disposal of Schiele. The exhibition, for which Schiele had also created the publicity poster, develops into a great artistic and financial success. Schiele takes possession of an additional new art studio. His pregnant wife Edith dies on 28th October due to the Spanish flu, followed three days later, on 31st October, by the artist himself, who is felled by the same epidemic.

64

Egon Schiele
Fighting, ca. 1910
aquarelle and gouache, 14,7 x 14 cm
Inv.Nr. 1802

65

Egon Schiele
Male Nude, 1912
lithograph, 42 x 21 cm
Inv.Nr. 388

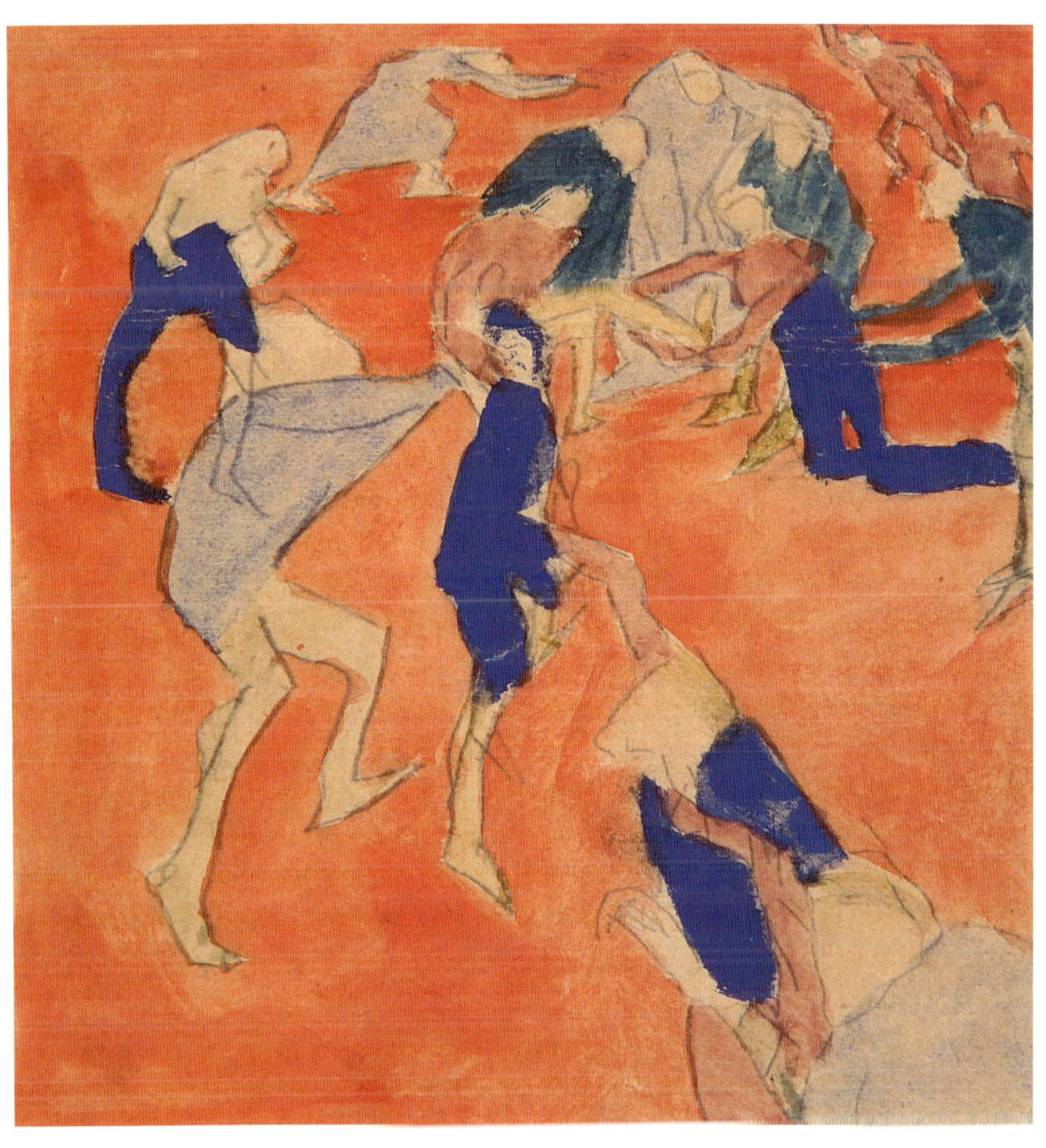

Cat. 64

105

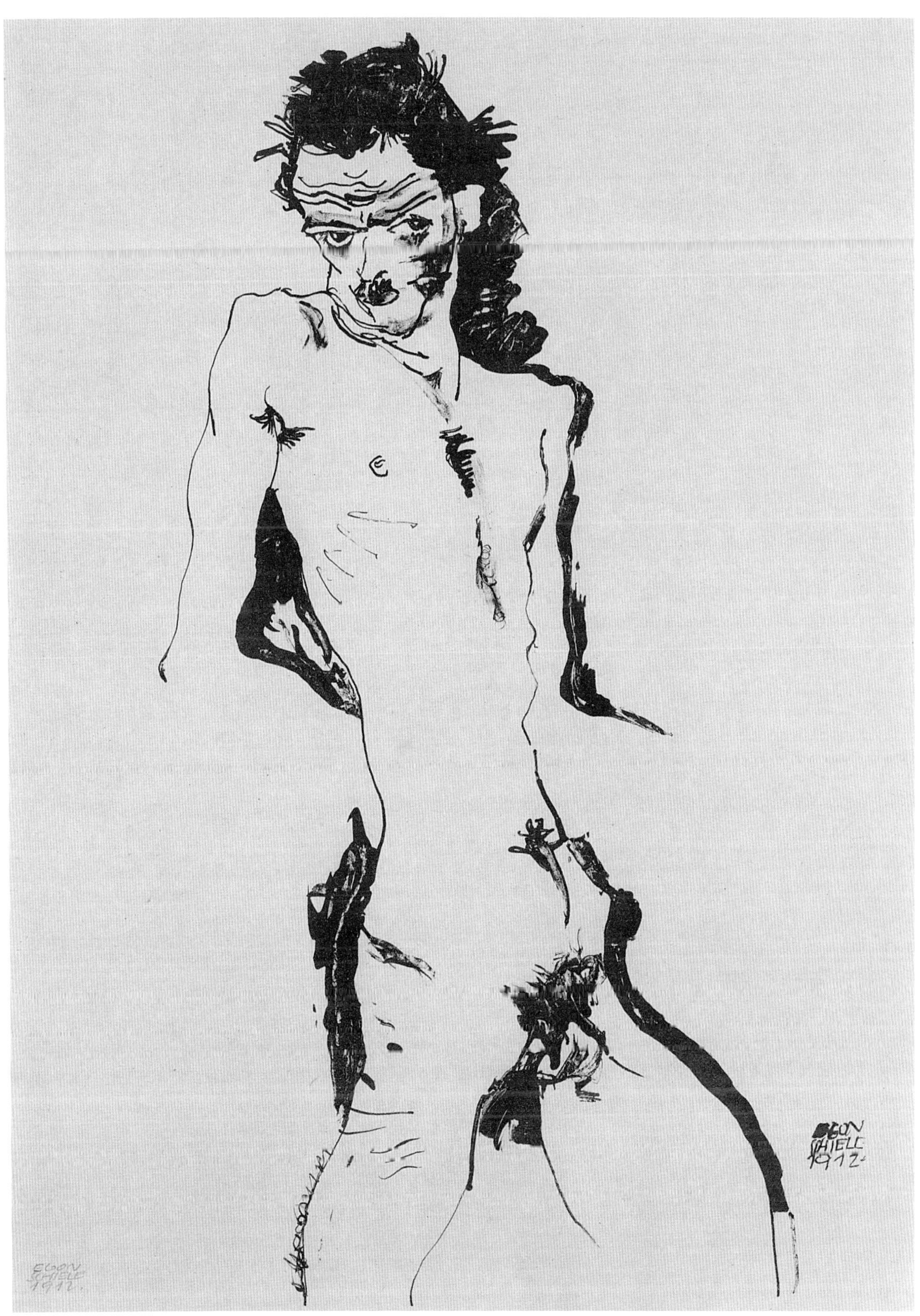

Wilhelm Thöny

Born on February 10, 1888, in Graz. Died on May 1, 1949 in New York.

Starting in 1908, the painter and graphic artist Wilhelm Thöny studied and worked with Gabriel Hackl and Angelo Jank at the Academy of Fine Arts in Munich. In 1913, together with Franz Marc and Albert Weissgerber, Thöny had a major part in the founding of the "Münchener Neue Secession".

He was drafted into military service during World War I. In 1923, five years after the end of the war, Thöny, together with Franz Silberbauer and Alfred Wickenburg, founded the "Grazer Secession".

His first stay in Paris in 1929 led him to turn away from German expressionism. His hitherto dark and gloomy colors started to become lighter and brighter, and his formerly pastose technique became less so. These changes, which were clearly evident by 1931, established a stylistic metamorphosis to spirited, poignant landscapes, and figural representations of fleeting grace and lightness.

In 1938, faced with the new political situation in Austria, the artist moved to New York, a city he had come to know back in 1933, and to which he had devoted a number of cityscapes of clearly determined line, yet highlighted by bursts of color. After coming to New York again, he no longer painted, but did mostly drawings, occasionally adding a touch of tempera.

On March 4, 1948, a tragic fire in a New York warehouse destroyed a major part of Thöny's lifetime oeuvre. Not much later, he himself passed away.

66

Wilhelm Thöny
Nun, about 1920
pen and ink with wash and light aquarelle,
22,5 x 31,5 cm
donation by Mrs. Thea Thöny
Inv.Nr. 2724

67

Wilhelm Thöny
Two Women, 1929
pencil, 27,3 x 21 cm
donation by Norli and Hellmut Czerny
Inv.Nr. 3371

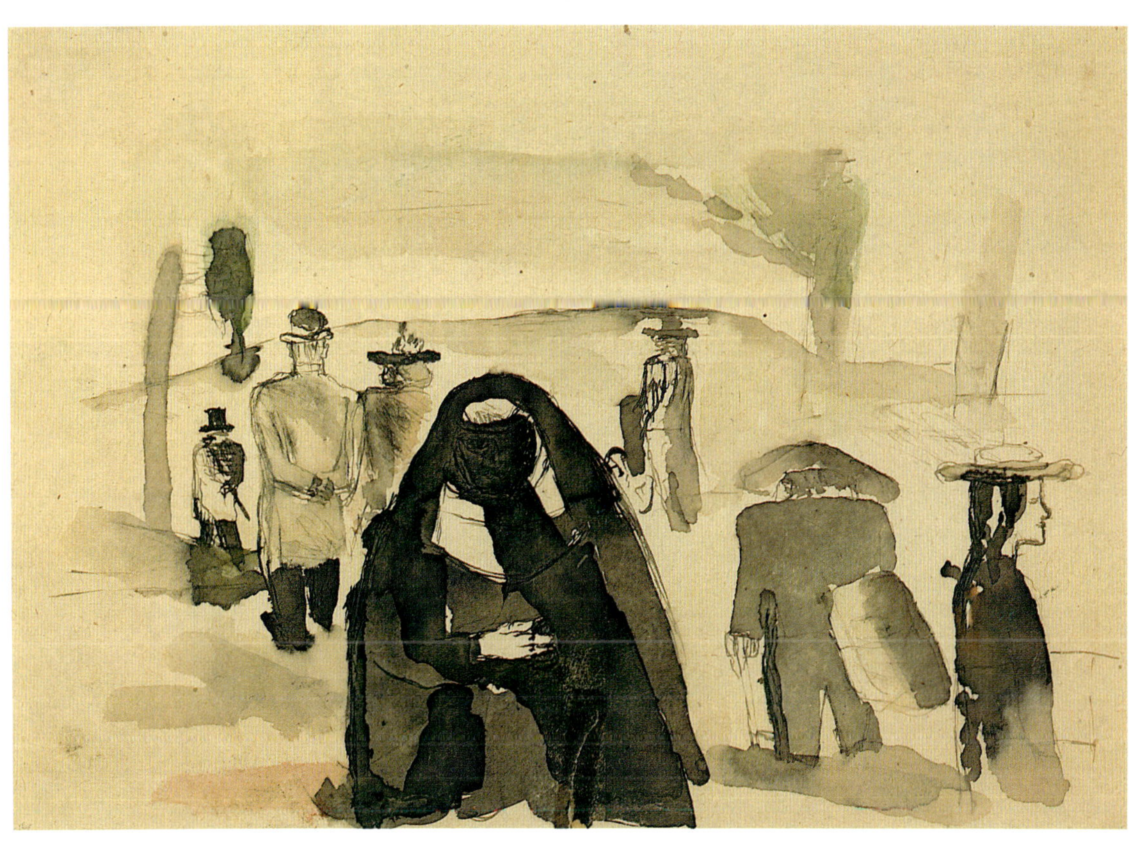

Cat. 66

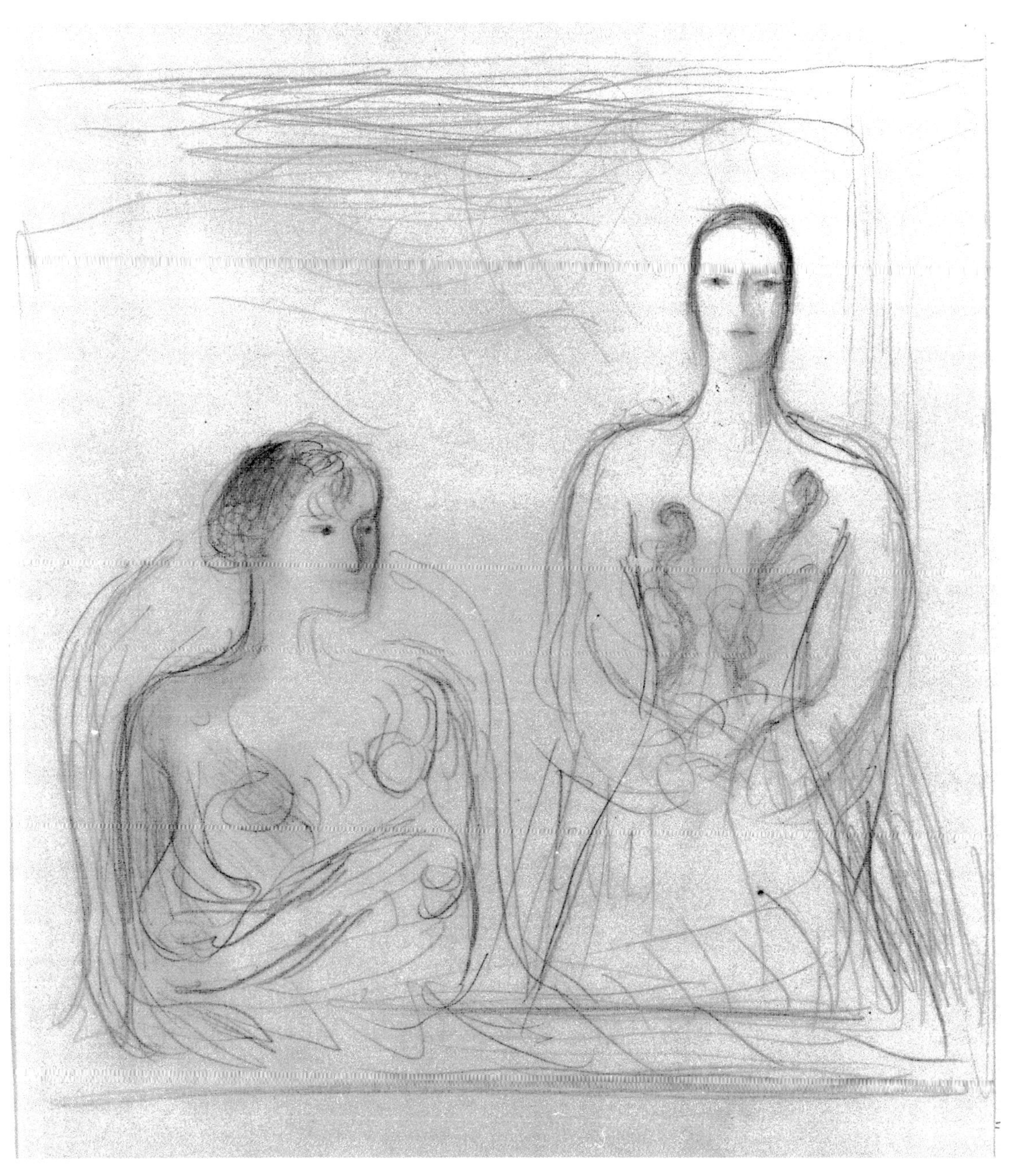

Cat. 67

Aloys Wach

1872   Born in Lambach; died 1940 in Braunau, Upper Austria. He was the second of altogether ten children of Anton and Anna Wachlmayr.

1904   Wach's father died, and his brother became legal guardian for the ten semiorphans. Aloys Wach became a member of the boys' choir of the Abbey of Lambach, attended a public school in Wels, and eventually became apprenticed to a businessman.

1909—1912   From 1909—1912 he attended two fine-arts schools in Vienna, yet, because of lack of money, was unable to graduate from either one of them. Similarly, he did not succed in passing the entrance exams of the Fine Arts Academies in Vienna and Munich, supposedly for lack of talent.

1912   He managed to get in touch with Herwarth Walden's radical and progressive group of artists "Sturm" in Berlin. Subsequently, Wach consistently worked for the periodical of the same name.

1913—1914   Wach attended the painting school of Knirr-Sailer in Munich, and established contact with the "Blaue Reiter" group. He stayed in Paris from 1913—1914 where he made the acquaintance of Amadeo Modigliani.

1914—1915   He stayed on the shores of the Ammersee (a large lake in Bavaria), in Stuttgart, and in Munich. In this period, he still signed his paintings "Wachlmayr" or "Wachlmeier".

1917   He was drafted and assigned to a company charged with administrative duties.

1918   Wach began to correspond with Egon Schiele.

1919   Together with his wife who hailed from Munich, Aloys Wach now settled near Braunau, Upper Austria.

1920   Adoption of a child. The family moved to Braunau.

1925   Wach received the "Staatspreis" (a high Austrian government award) for his "Bauernzyklus", a series of works having farm life as their common subject matter.

1926   He declines to accept the position of professor at the Berlin academy he has been offered.

1935   He and his family move into a row house in Braunau which he himself owns.

1940   Aloys Wach died of tuberculosis (as did two of his brothers before him).

68

Aloys Wach
Recycling Female Nude, 1914
graphite pencil on tracing paper,
23,2 x 34,3 cm
Inv.Nr. 1998

69

Aloys Wach
The Son, from the cycle The Lost Son, 1920
woodcut, 22 x 37,5 to 55,5 x 46 cm
Inv.Nr. 2825

70

Aloys Wach
*The Lost Son, from the
Cycle The Lost Son, 1920*
woodcut, 27 x 26,7 to 55,5 x 46 cm
Inv.Nr. 2826

71

Aloys Wach
*Son and Girl, from the Cycle The Lost Son,
1920*
woodcut, 37,5 x 37 to 55,5 x 46 cm
Inv.Nr. 2829

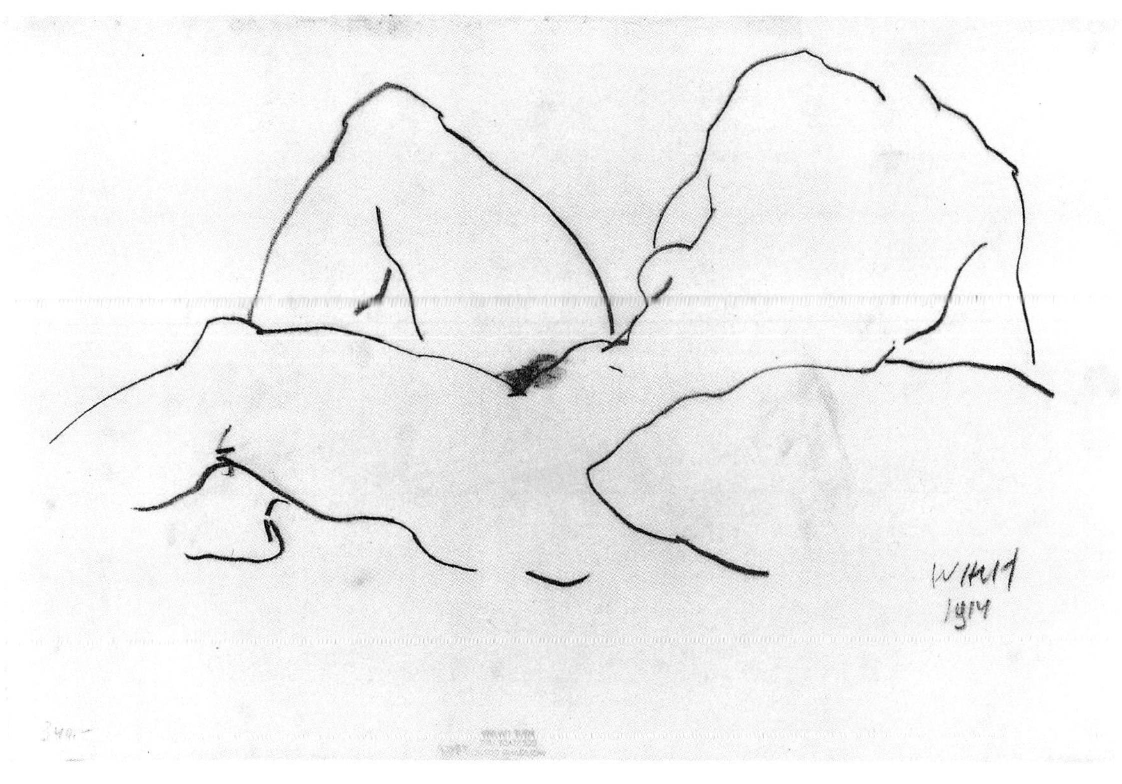

Cat. 68

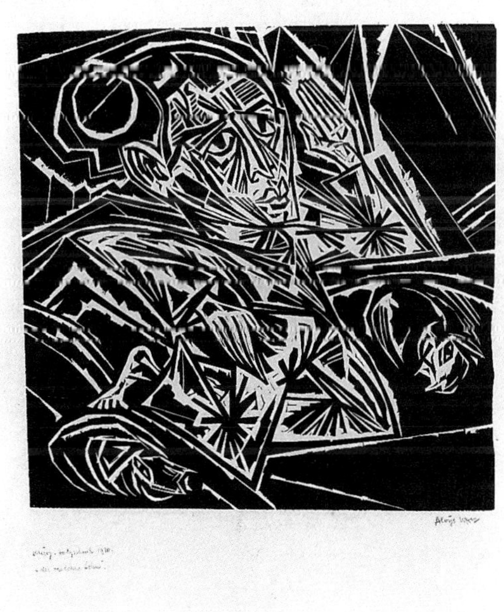

Cat. 70

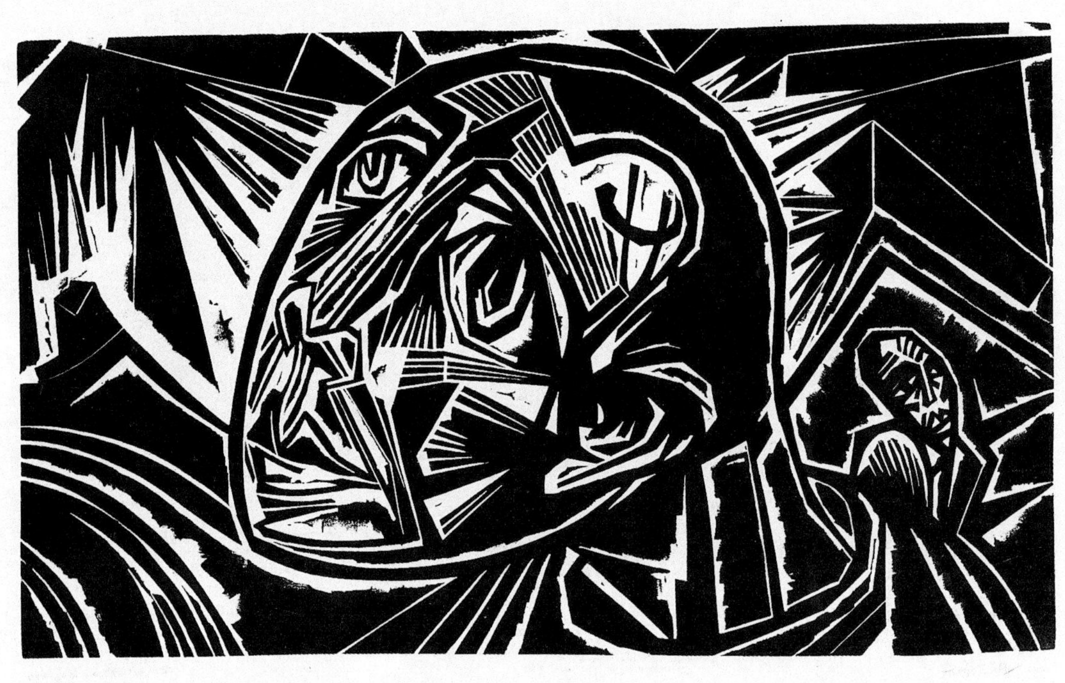

Cat. 69

114

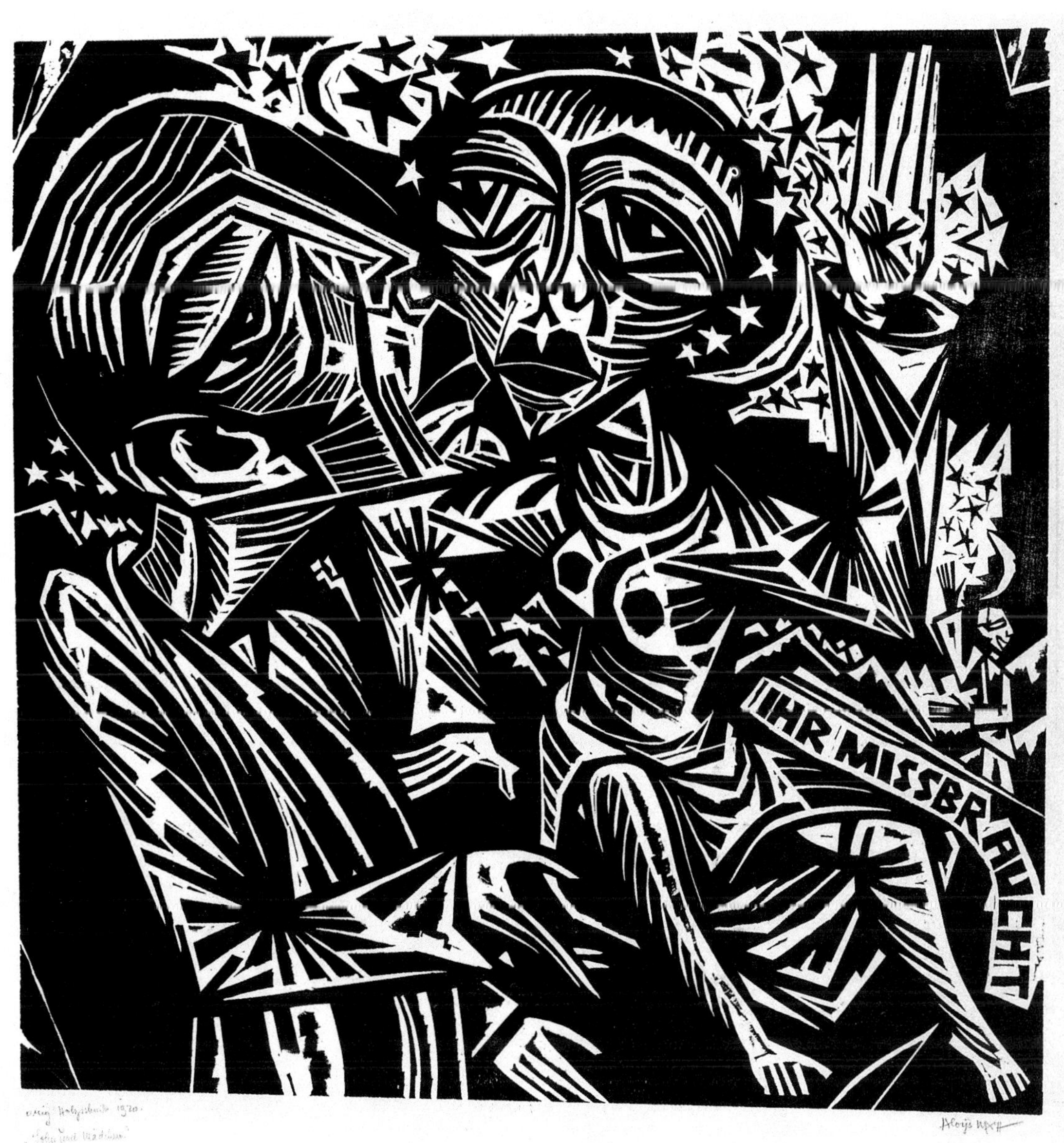

IHR MISSBRAUCHT

Alfons Walde

Born Oberndorf, Tyrol, 1891
died Kitzbühel, Tyrol, 1958
Son of a Tyrolean primary school principal. 1910 began his architectural studies at the Technische Hochschule (technical university) in Vienna. 1912—14 Herbert Boeckl as fellow-student. Concurrently studied painting.
1914—18 military service with the Tiroler Kaiserschützen.
1925 represented at the "Biennial" in Rome. 1926 member of the Wiener Künstlerhaus. Numerous exhibitions at home and abroad.
Initially influenced by Albin Egger-Lienz whose formal aspects he evaluated without carrying over his inherent heaviness and tragic attitude. At the same time influenced by Schiele and Klimt's decorative-ornamental paintings. Decorative still lifes and mundane portraits of females prevail in his early work. Later he immersed himself in tradition and life of his native Tyrolean country and depicted the life of Tyrolean farmers, their positive disposition being in stark contrast to the hopeless and depressive mood of Albin Egger-Lienz. In colorful and thick brush-strokes Walde celebrated the beauty of his native landscape. Posters of the interwar period with homey winter landscapes and advertising winter sports furthered his international renown.

72
Alfons Walde
Figural Composition, before 1920
oil on paper, 21,1 x 34,3 cm
Inv.Nr. 3564

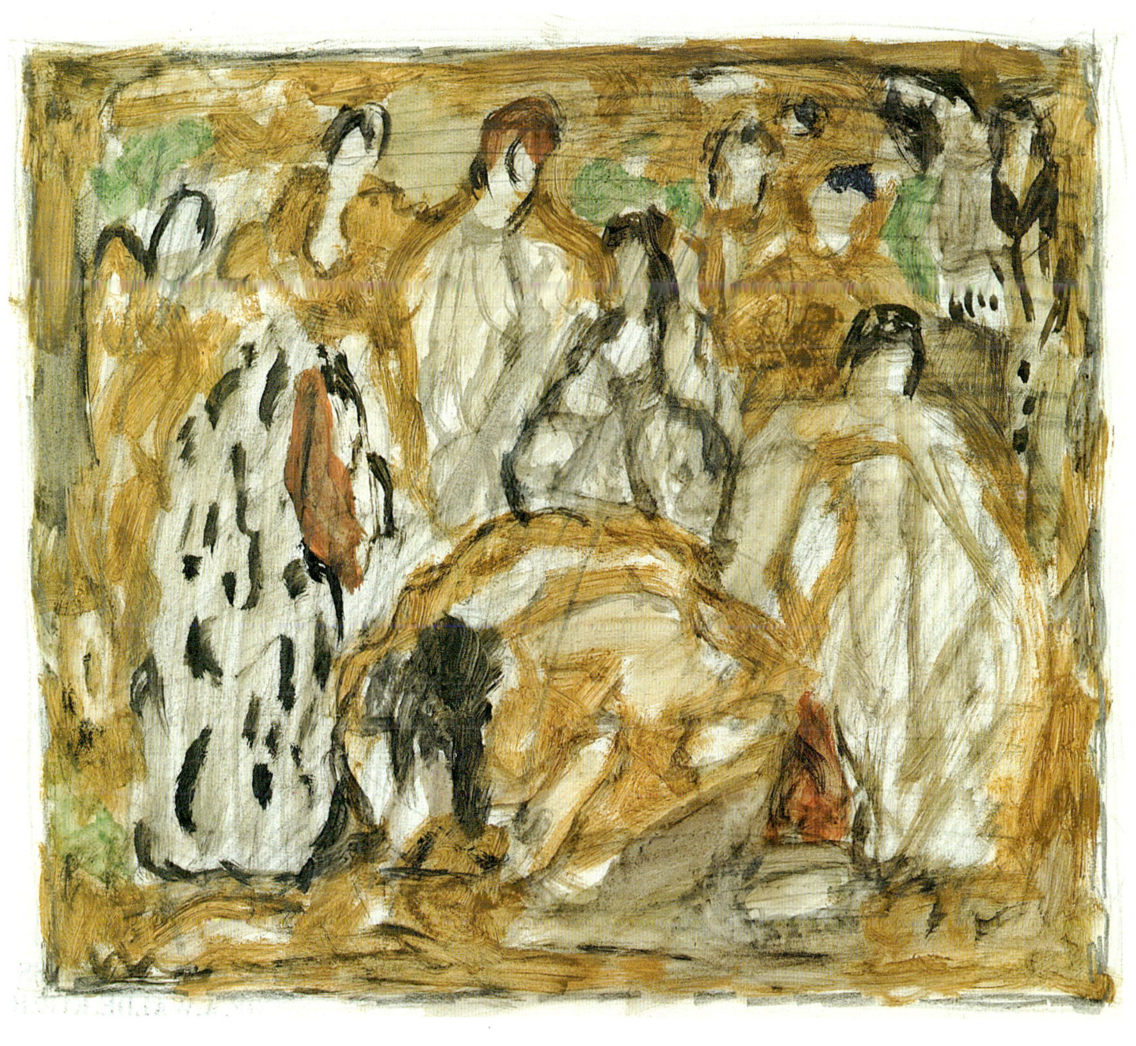

Cat. 72

117

Franz von Zülow

Born Vienna, 1883
died Vienna, 1963
1901 attended Graphische Lehr- und Versuchsanstalt (graphics school), Vienna. 1903—07 studied at the Wiener Kunstgewerbeschule (applied arts). Soon after he produced his first decorative works for the Wiener Werkstätte. 1908 member of the Wiener Secession. In the twenties he created numerous blueprints for the decoration of furniture, porcelain, and textiles. 1925 gold medal of the International Exhibition of Arts and Crafts in Paris. 1939 painted the pyrotechnic security curtain for the stage of the Akademietheater, Vienna. He also produced a rich oeuvre of paintings and graphic art. 1943/44 in spite of many awards and honorary degrees the Nazis banned all his activities.
Landscapes were Zülow's chief topic; his colors are expressive and on occasion the narration is deliberately simple, almost naive. He liked to experiment with graphic techniques; from 1907 he developed the paper-cut-stencil method which he patented.

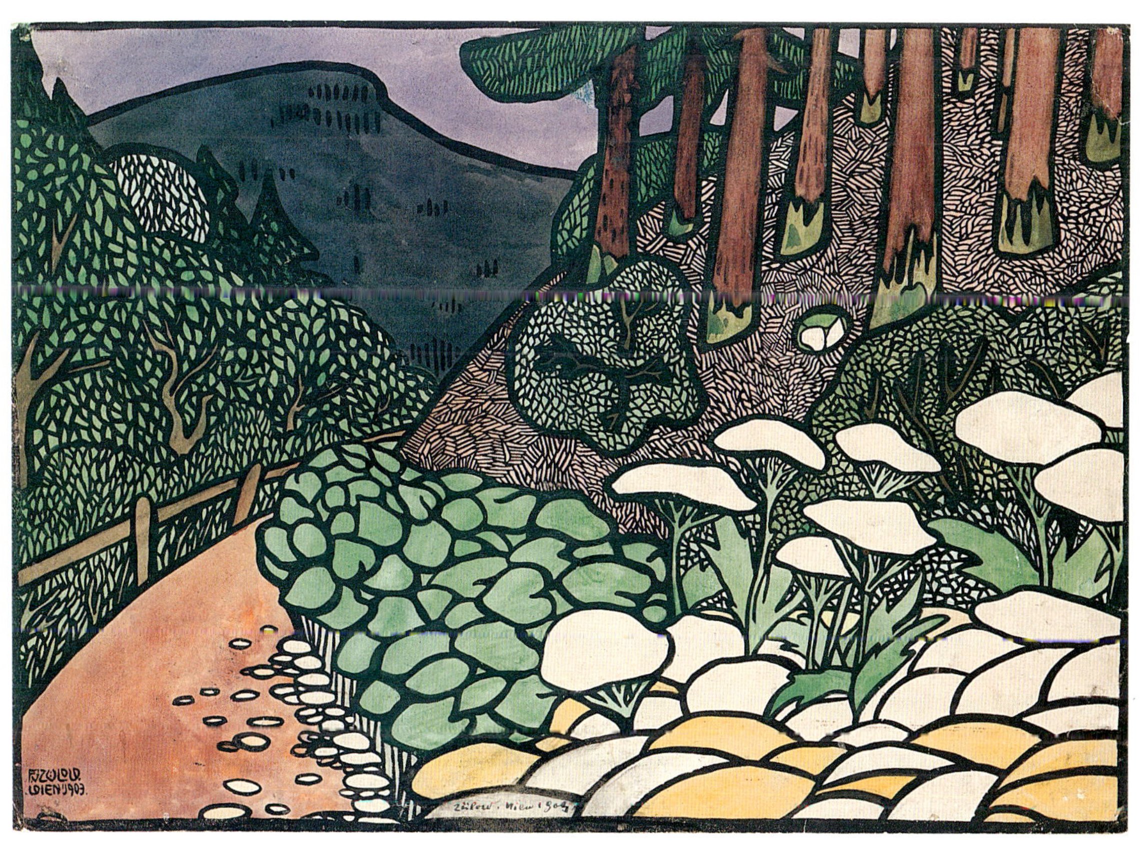

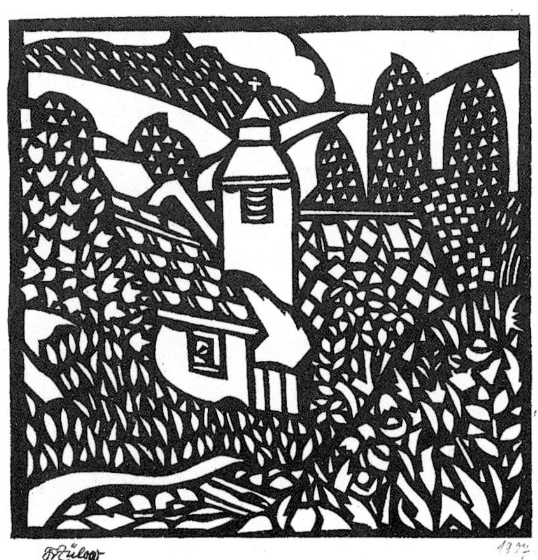

Cat. 76

73

Franz Zülow
Forest with Hemlock Trees, 1903
ink and tempera on paper, 32 x 45 cm
Inv.Nr. 2997

74

Franz Zülow
Furrows, about 1904/05
paper stencil print with aquarelle,
34,6 x 31,4 cm
Zülow Donation
Inv.Nr. 4376

75

Franz Zülow
Nursery, 1906
paper stencil print, 29,5 x 29,5 to 41 x 40,5 cm
Inv.Nr. 1763

76

Franz Zülow
Church with Cypress Trees, 1907
paper stencil print, 29,4 x 29,4 cm
Inv.Nr. 1762

77

Franz Zülow
*The Pulkau River near Haugsdorf with
Two Willows, 1908*
paper stencil print,
30,8 x 30,5 to 40,5 x 40,5 cm
Inv.Nr. 1766

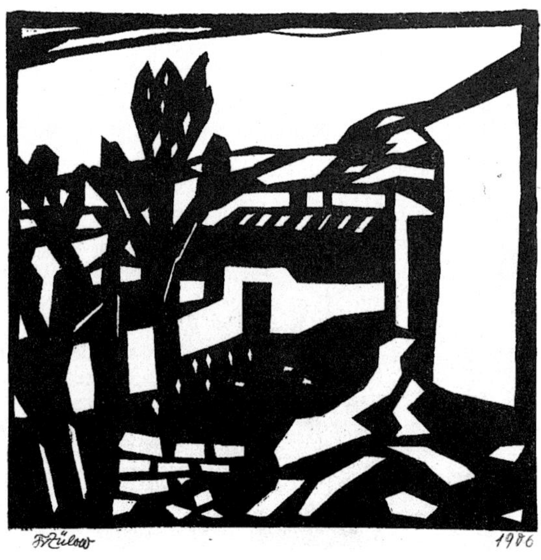

Cat. 75

120

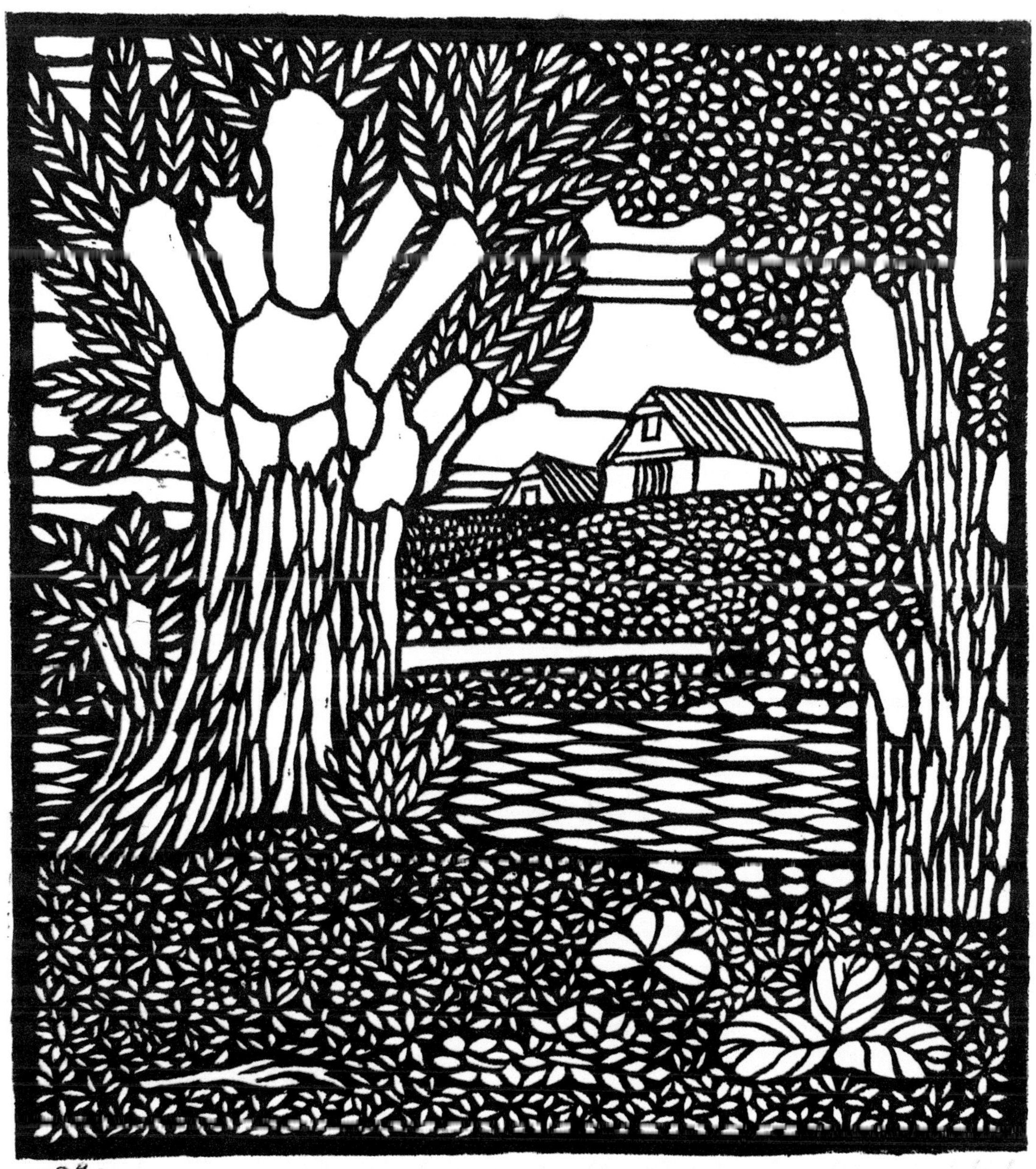

Cat. 77

121

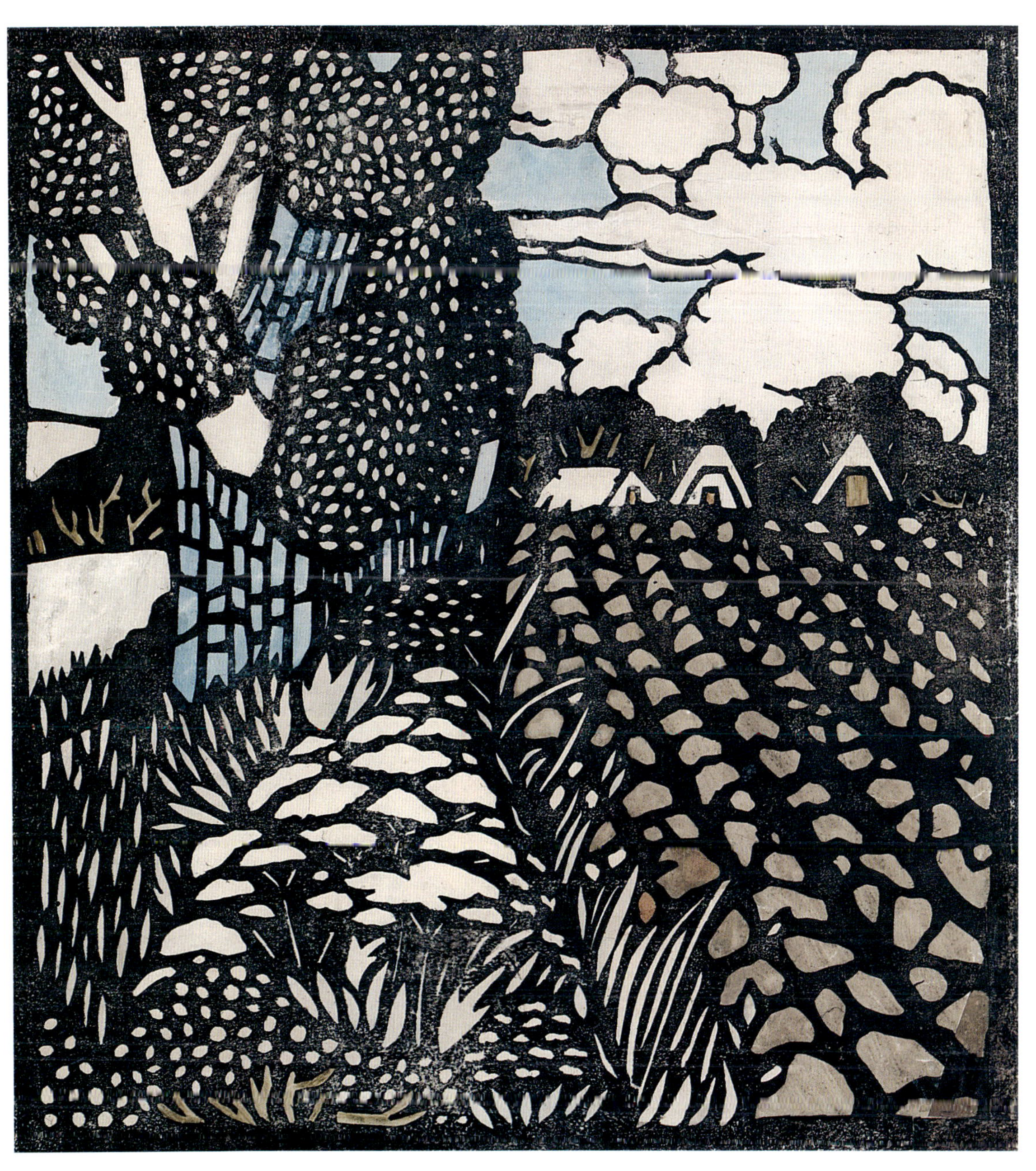

Cat. 74

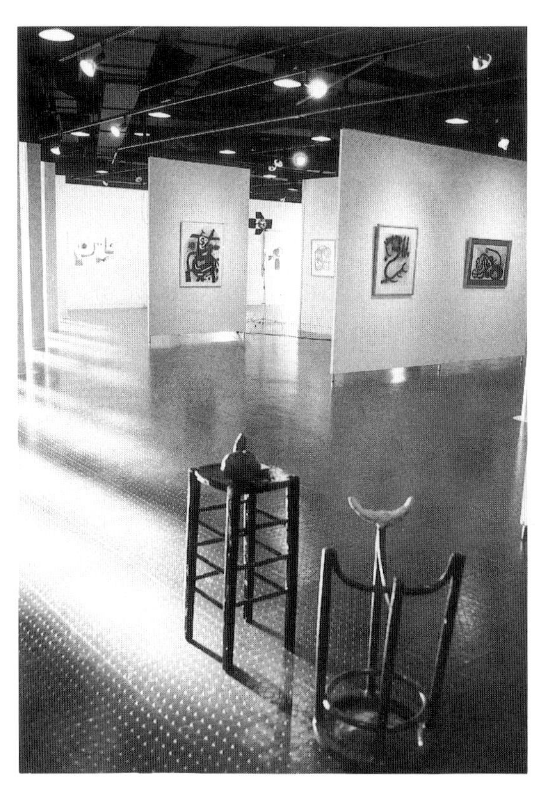

Miro-Exhibition, 1979

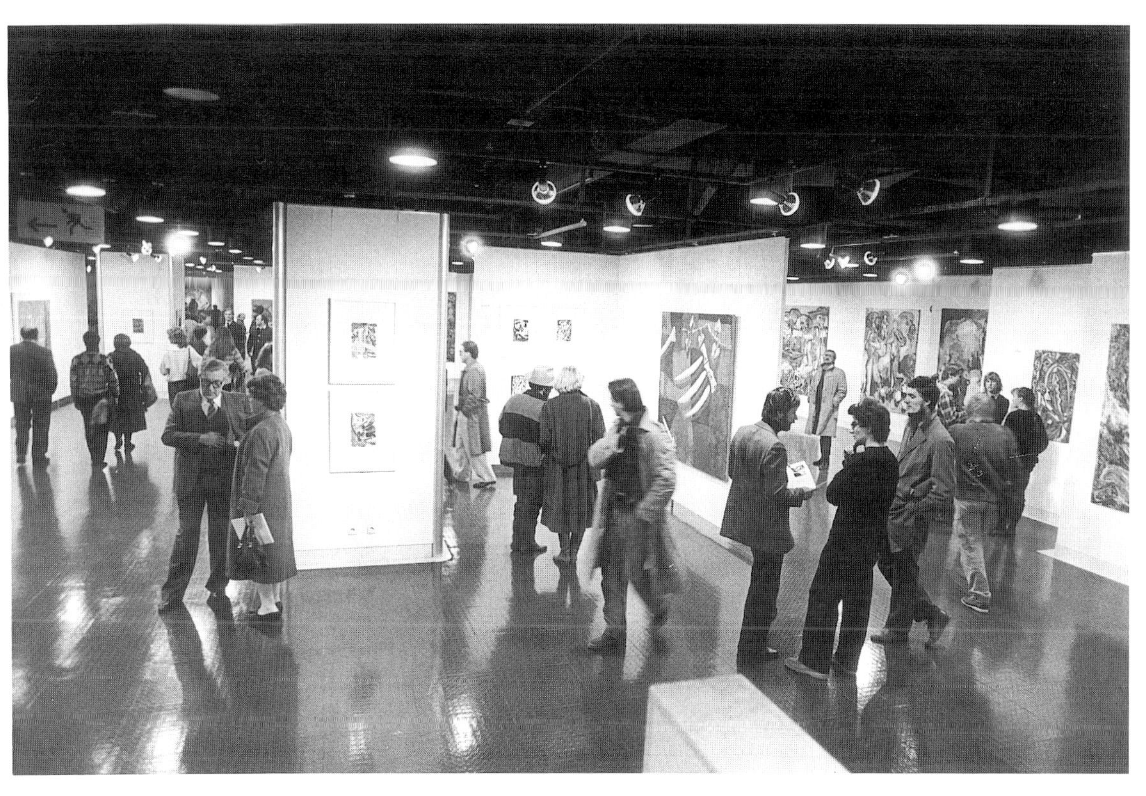

Neue Galerie der Stadt Linz, Austria

Contents

Published

1990 on the occasion of an exhibition organized by the Smithsonian Institution Traveling Exhibition Service and the Neue Galerie der Stadt Linz, Austria.

Catalogue designed by Peter Baum.

Printed by Landesverlag, Linz.

Photolithos by Laska-Repro, Linz.

All works from the Collection of the Neue Galerie der Stadt Linz.

Photographs from the archives of the Neue Galerie der Stadt Linz.

Frontispiece: Gustav Klimt, pencil 1914.

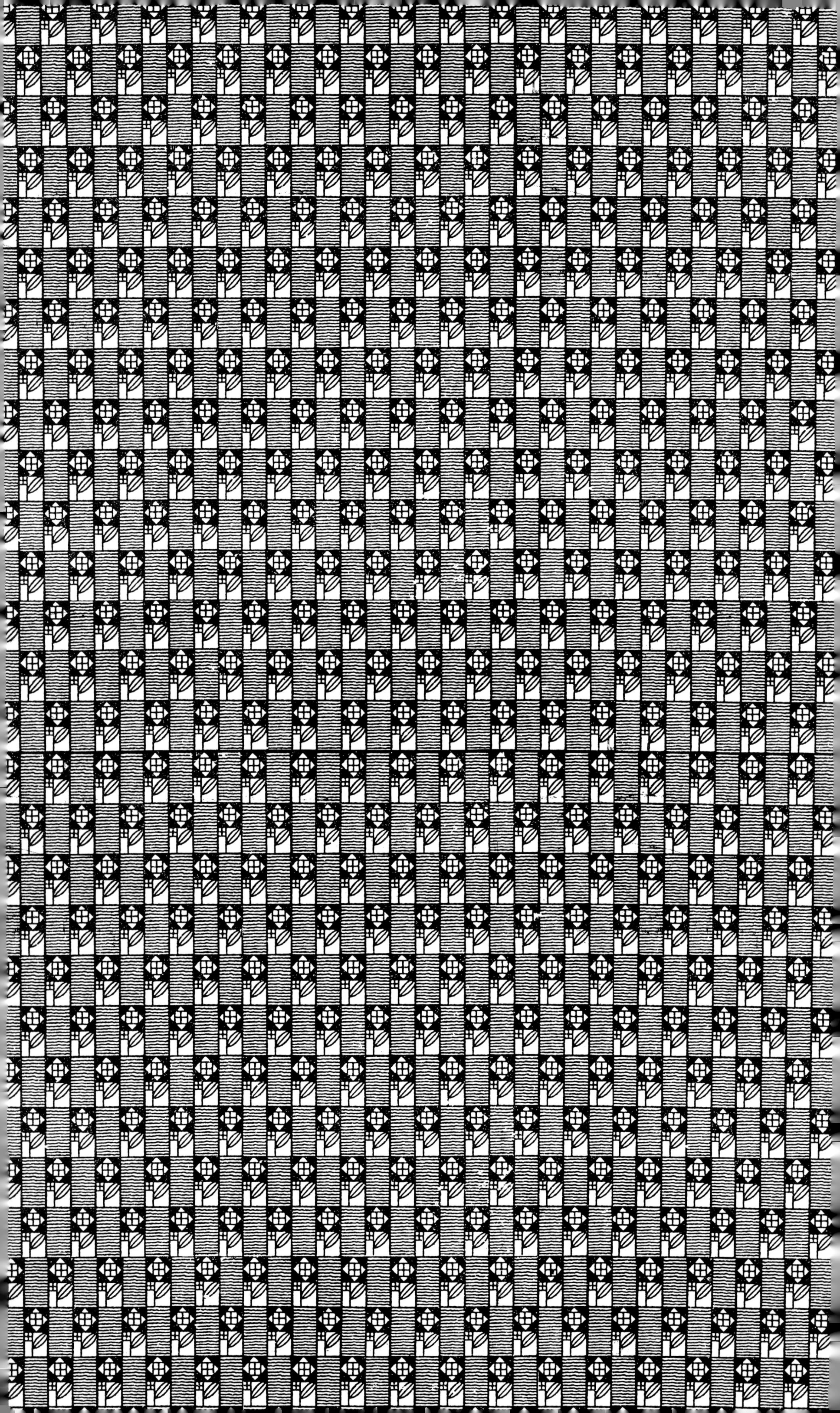